The Reason We Are Here
いま求められる
世界正義
私たちがここにいる理由

大川隆法
Ryuho Okawa

2019年10月6日
ザ ウェスティン ハーバー キャッスル
トロント カンファレンス センターにて

いま求められる世界正義

—The Reason We Are Here
私たちがここにいる理由 —

Preface

The main content of this book is the English lecture that I gave on October 6, 2019 (Canada time), to commemorate the 33rd anniversary of Happy Science and my giving of over 3,000 lectures.

It also includes the answers to three questions from the Q&A session given on the day of the lecture, as well as my replies to the questions that I gave after returning to Japan from two activists who are working for the freedom of Hong Kong and an activist who is working for the freedom of Uyghur who are all living in Canada.

My answers are related to Canada, so I could not speak enough, but I tried to talk about what is "world justice".

In Japan, after six months since my lecture in Japan, the Asahi newspaper, who originally supported mainland China, clearly criticized the Hong Kong

まえがき

本書は、2019年10月6日（カナダ時間）に、幸福の科学立宗33周年と、私の説法回数3000回突破を記念して、トロントで行った英語講演を基調としたものである。

同時に、会場で受けた3つの質問への答えと、講演終了後に頂いた、カナダ在住の香港解放の活動家2人と、ウイグル解放の活動家の質問に、帰国後、お答えした内容を併録している。

カナダという国をからめての回答になっているので、言葉は十分尽くせてないが、「世界正義」の所在を説いたつもりである。

日本では、国内での私の説法に遅れること約半年、中国本土の味方と思われていた朝日新聞が、11月の社説で、香港での警察の暴力の行きすぎを批判し、デモをし

3

police's excessive brutality in their November editorial. It showed that Asahi newspaper supports the people of Hong Kong and the students who are demonstrating. The Japanese administration is not taking a clear stance, whether that's because they're thinking about President Xi Jinping's visit to Japan and hosting the Tokyo Olympics next year. The opposition parties are also avoiding this Hong Kong issue.

All of the answers and keys are in this book.

This is a fight between the atheistic, materialistic country and the faithful people of Hong Kong and Uyghur.

My thinking is to lead the Hong Kong Revolution to a bloodless revolution in mainland China. Even for the 1.4 billion people of China, it's a way to happiness for them to acquire faith, fundamental human rights, democracy, and freedom. And, it's also the royal road to prosperity.

ている民衆・学生側に立つことを明らかにした。日本政府は、来年の習近平氏の来日と東京オリンピックの開催への配慮からか、態度を明確にせず、野党も香港問題から逃げている。

　全ての答えとヒントは本書にある。

　無神論・唯物論の国家 対、信仰を持つ、香港やウイグルの人々の戦いである。

　私の考えは、香港革命を、中国本土の無血革命につなげていくことである。14億人の中国国民にとっても、信仰、基本的人権、民主主義、自由が手に入ることは、幸福への道ではなかろうか。そして繁栄への王道ではなかろうか。

I don't want Japan to be a country that easily accepts the law of the jungle and thinks about economic profit only. I pray that Japan becomes a country of over five percent economic growth and a God-believing country again, and acquires the power to change the worst totalitarian dictatorship since Hitler into a peaceful and democratic one. And, I want to realize the day in which the people of Hong Kong, Uyghur, Tibet, Inner Mongolia, and others are freed from fear. I strongly hope so.

Nov. 15, 2019

Master & CEO of Happy Science Group

Ryuho Okawa

私は日本という国が、弱肉強食を単純に肯定し、経済的利益ばかりを考える国にはなってほしくない。日本が再び5％以上の強い経済成長力と、神への信仰を持つ国となり、ヒットラー以来の全体主義独裁国家を平和な民主主義国家に変える力を持つことを祈っている。そして香港、ウイグル、チベット、内モンゴルなどの人々が恐怖から解放される日を実現したいと、強く願っている。

2019 年 11 月 15 日

幸福の科学グループ創始者兼総裁

大川隆法

Contents

Preface 2

Chapter 1 The Reason We Are Here

1 My Impression of Toronto 18

2 Canada is in Its Term of Election
for the Next Prime Minister 22

3 Canada Should Decide Pivotal Things 26
Too much liberalism leads to the weakness of the country ... 26
Even Canada sent a battleship near Hong Kong 30

4 What I Want to Say about Global Warming 32
Global warming has been the trend for the last 10,000 years 32
Behind global warming theory lies communist thinking 36

5 Real Responsibility Means World Justice 40
We must stop the poverty and war in the world...................... 40
Deciding nothing means no responsibilities,
not tolerance... 42

6 The Common Base of Prosperity of
Taiwan and Hong Kong 44
China has not experienced real democracy................................ 44
The starting point of Umbrella Revolution and
Hong Kong Revolution 46

目　次

まえがき 3

第1章　私たちがここにいる理由

1　トロントの印象について 19

2　次期首相の選挙期間中のカナダ 23

3　カナダは肝心なことを判断すべき 27
行きすぎたリベラリズムは国力を弱める 27
カナダさえ香港近辺に軍艦を派遣 31

4　地球温暖化説について 33
温暖化は1万年前から続いている 33
温暖化説の背後にある共産主義的考え方 37

5　本当の「責任」とは世界正義を担うこと 41
世界の貧困と戦争の問題に取り組むべき 41
決断を避けるのは「寛容」ではなく「無責任」 43

6　台湾と香港の「繁栄」の基盤とは 45
中国は本物の民主主義を経験していない 45
雨傘革命と香港革命の原点 47

7 China's Ethnic Suppression and Totalitarian Regime .. 50

Democracy and freedom will make China
greater than as it is 50

Checkpoint: belief in God and fundamental rights 52

8 God is Not Dead 56

9 After Visiting the Gay Town in Toronto 60

A lost spirit appeared in my hotel room..................................... 60

LGBT matter in Christian and Japanese societies..................... 62

10 The Reason We Are Here 64

The human soul is made of a group of souls........................... 64

The human soul can be born as male or female....................... 68

11 In This Materialistic World, Be Spiritual 70

7 中国の民族弾圧と全体主義体制 51
「民主」と「自由」が中国をより素晴らしくする 51
そこに「信仰」と「基本的人権」はあるか 53

8 神は死んでいない 57

9 トロントのゲイタウンを訪れて 61
ホテルにやってきた「迷える霊」 61
キリスト教社会と日本に広がる LGBT 問題 63

10 「私たちがここにいる理由」 65
人間の魂はグループを作っている 65
人は男女どちらに生まれることもできる 69

11 物質世界にあって霊的に生きる 71

Chapter 2 Q&A Session

1 New Faith to Spread in North America 76

Canada has a lot of hidden power 76

Happy Science accepts believers of other religions 78

God Thoth governs North America 84

2 Helping Patients Who Suffer from Drug Abuse 88

Pray for the power from heaven 90

3 The Real Meaning of Golden Age 96

Chapter 3 Master Okawa's Answers
to Canadian Activists

1 Interviews with Three Activists 104

**2 Answer to Ms. Fung: Advice to
Supporters of Hong Kong Democratic Protests** 120

China's strategy to change the opinion of the world 124

Be patient, and continue to protest using peaceful means 130

Look at the situation from the objective view of
an outside country 136

The world is following my design 138

A complicated strategy to surround China
through opinion and economy 142

第2章　質疑応答

1　北米に広めるべき新たな信仰とは 77
カナダは大きな力を秘めている 77

幸福の科学は他宗の信者も受け入れている 79

北米を司る神「トス」の存在 85

2　薬物乱用患者を救うには 89
天上界の力を求めよ 91

3　「ゴールデン・エイジ」の本当の意味とは 97

第3章　カナダの活動家の質問に答える

1　活動家3人のインタビュー 105

2　ファン氏への回答
　　——香港の民主化デモ勢力へのアドバイス 121

世界の意見を変えようとする中国の戦略 125

忍耐し、平和的デモの継続を 131

他国の視点で情勢の客観視を 137

世界は私のデザイン通りに動いている 139

言論面や経済面も含む複雑な「中国包囲戦略」 143

3 Answer to Ms. Sheng: The Plan to Realize
  a Free China within the Next 10 Years 152

  Canada should adopt the Benjamin Franklin spirit 158

  A long timespan of planning to change the Earth 164

  The danger of a surveillance society ruled by AI 170

  Above economy and politics lies God's justice 176

4 Answer to Ms. Turdush:
  A Message to Fighters Who Have Faith in God 182

  The world is now changing after I gave lectures
  in Germany and Taiwan 186

  The end of China: its economic collapse 192

  Elohim's promise to His people of Uyghur 196

5 God's Plan and Our Mission 200

★ All three sessions were conducted in English. The Japanese text is a translation.

3 盛雪氏への回答 —— 次の 10 年で
「自由な中国」を実現するための計画は 153

カナダに「ベンジャミン・フランクリン精神」を 159

地球の変化は長いスパンで計画されている 165

AI による監視社会の危険性 171

経済や政治の上に「神の正義」がある 177

4 トールダッシュ氏への回答
—— 戦う信仰者たちへのメッセージ 183

ドイツと台湾での説法が世界を変えつつある 187

経済崩壊が「中国の終わり」の時 193

ウイグル人の神エローヒムの約束 197

5 神の計画と私たちの使命 201

※本書は、英語で収録された法話と質疑応答に和訳を付けたものです。

第1章

The Reason We Are Here
（私たちがここにいる理由）

October 6, 2019 at The Westin Harbour Castle, Toronto, Canada
（2019年10月6日　カナダ・トロント、ザ・ウェスティン・ハーバー・キャッスルにて）

1 My Impression of Toronto

Hi. Hello, Toronto. Nice to meet you. Thank you. Thank you. Thank you very much.

OK. Yeah, this is my first lecture in Canada. A few days ago, I got through the airport gate, and one of the agents asked me, "Why are you here? Please teach me your purpose of journey." I answered, "I have one lecture in Toronto." She asked me, "What lecture is that?" I answered, "The theme is, 'The Reason We Are Here'." [*Audience laughs.*] She cannot understand my purpose, so I said, "Ah, except in Canada, I'm very famous." I said so. This is a reason we are here.

Yeah, it's the first time for me, "Who is Ryuho Okawa?" she asked. Even in India, with more than one billion population, they know about me. "Oh, I saw you on TV or poster or like that." Or, even in Hong Kong, the lady at the bookstore knew about

1　トロントの印象について

　トロントのみなさん、こんにちは。はじめまして。ありがとう。ありがとう。ありがとうございます。

　はい。これが私のカナダでの初説法になります。数日前に空港でゲートを通ったのですが、職員の一人から、「なぜ来られたのですか。旅行の目的を教えてください」と聞かれましたので、「トロントで講演をするのですが」と答えました。彼女が「何の講演ですか」と聞くので、「テーマは "The Reason We Are Here"（私たちがここにいる理由）です」と答えました（会場笑）。彼女が私の目的を理解できないので、私は言いました。「ああ、カナダ以外では私は非常に有名なんですけどね」。だからこそ、〝私たちはここにいる〟わけですね。

　「大川隆法とは誰ですか」と聞かれたのは初めてです。インドですら、人口10億人以上ですが、私は知られています。「ああ、テレビかポスターか何かであなたを見ました」と。また香港でも、書店の女性が私を知っていましたので、「一緒に写真を撮っていただけますか」と

me, and I asked her, "Would you take a photo with me?" and she hesitated. "No. In Hong Kong, it's not permitted," she said.

OK, OK. This is Canada, so I want to start a new type of lecture. I stayed for two or three days already, and the impression of Canada is very gentle, tender, and kind. And I've never met a really bad person in this country because of few population, maybe. But the country is very huge and your resources are very fertile, and you may have a big dream, "you can".

お願いしましたが、彼女は尻込みして「いえ、香港では
それは許可されていませんので」と答えました。

　オーケー、ここはカナダですので、新しいタイプの説
法を始めたいと思います。すでに二、三日滞在していま
すが、カナダは非常に優しく、穏やかで、親切であると
いう印象を受けました。この国では、人口が少ないせい
かもしれませんが、本当に悪い人にはまだ会っていませ
ん。国土が非常に広大で、資源もたいへん豊かですので、
皆様は「自分たちにはできる」という大きな夢を持って
いるのではないかと思います。

2 Canada is in Its Term of Election for the Next Prime Minister

And this is the term of election for next prime minister, so you are very busy in reality. I was asked about that. "Mr. Trudeau or Mr. Scheer, which do you like?" I cannot answer exactly. Both are good. Both are good leaders for Canada. But I just feel that, Mr. Trudeau said in his book, I mean *Common Ground*, "In Canada, Trudeau means responsibility." He said in that book. Trudeau is a famous name in Canada, and it's 'responsibility'. How about, then, Mr. Scheer? He said nothing about that, but he wants to get some responsibility about Canada.

We are not so huge in members in Canada, so I won't speak too much regarding next elections, but to tell the truth, I think Prime Minister Trudeau is like what we think, "This is Canadian-like thinking," he dispatches such kind of thinking. He is

2 次期首相の選挙期間中のカナダ

　今は、次の首相の選挙期間中ですので、実際、非常に忙しい時期です。私も「トルドーさんとシーアさんの、どちらがいいでしょうか」と聞かれましたが、はっきり答えることはできません。どちらも良い方です。どちらもカナダにとって立派な指導者ですが、私の感じといたしましては、トルドーさんは著書の『コモン・グラウンド』で、「『トルドー』とは、カナダでは『責任』を意味する」と言っています。トルドーはカナダでは有名な名前で、責任のことであるというわけです。ではシーアさんはどうなのかに関しては、何も書かれていませんが、彼はカナダについて一定の責任を負うつもりでいるわけです。

　カナダでは私たちのメンバーはそれほど多くありませんので、次の選挙についてあまり多くを語ることはいたしませんが、率直な考えをお話しするとすれば、トルドー首相は、私たちが「いかにもカナダ的な考え方である」と思うような考え方を打ち出していると思います。非常

very gentle, and he is very kind and tolerant, and he is liberal-oriented. The final one… [*Smiling, he stops the audience from clapping*] No, stop. [*Audience laughs.*] The conclusion is quite different, so never praise about that.

But the final one, "liberal" is a deep word in that meaning. And in a common sense, to be liberal is not so bad. For example, if you use the word "liberal" in the totalitarian regime, you can destroy that type of country by the word "tolerant" or "liberal" or "democracy" or "freedom of speech" or "freedom of expression" or "freedom of political actions."

に優しく親切で寛容な方であり、「リベラル」の傾向が
あります。この最後の点に関しては……（会場から拍手
が起こりかけたのを笑顔で押しとどめて）いえ、おやめ
ください（会場笑）。結論はまったく違いますので、こ
こは、ほめるところではありません。

　この最後の「リベラル」（自由主義的）という言葉に
は深い意味があります。普通の意味では、「リベラルで
ある」のは、それほど悪いことではありません。たとえ
ば、全体主義体制のなかで「リベラル」という言葉を使
う場合は、「寛容」「リベラル」「民主主義」「言論の自由」
「表現の自由」「政治行動の自由」などの言葉によって、
そうした国を倒すことが可能です。

3 Canada Should Decide Pivotal Things

Too much liberalism leads to the weakness of the country

You already can guess what I want to say. Yeah, I've heard that recently in Toronto, there was a collision regarding demonstration for Hong Kong problem. In Canada's opinion, if Canadian people are living in Hong Kong, they will support Hong Kong people, I guess so, because Canadian people maybe think that the gigantic Beijing China is a very totalitarian regime, and they easily deprive the freedom of the people. I think so. But I've heard that the demonstration made a great confusion because of the students from mainland China, and it's very famous worldwide, but I think the students from China have patriotism for their nation. I can understand about that.

3　カナダは肝心なことを判断すべき

行きすぎたリベラリズムは国力を弱める

　もう、私の申し上げたいことはお察しいただけるで
しょう。最近トロントで香港問題に関するデモがあり、
そこで衝突があったと聞きました。カナダの意見として
は、カナダ人が香港に住んでいたら香港の人たちを支持
するのではないかと思います。カナダの方たちは、「巨
大な中国政府はきわめて全体主義的な体制であり、人々
から平気で自由を奪う」と考えていると思われるからで
す。しかし、そのデモは中国本土からの留学生たちのせ
いで大混乱に陥ったそうで、それが世界中に知れわたり
ましたが、中国からの留学生にも自分の国への愛国心が
あるのだと思います。その点は理解できます。

3 Canada Should Decide Pivotal Things

But the Canadian people want to teach them that, "We are not the United States of America, but we are living next door to the United States of America, so we have almost the same tendency." Only to think too much tolerance and too much liberalism easily leads to weakness of this country. Canada doesn't have such kind of strongness of the United States, but the weakness, or just easily wants to be followers of strong countries. This is a problem of Canada. I guess so.

It's also the problem of Japan. I am the Founder and CEO of Happy Science Group, and we have a political party. Its name is Happiness Realization Party, in Japan. Only Happiness Realization Party made a demonstration in Japan for freedom of Hong Kong. Almost all Japanese people are just watching because they can understand the tragedy of Hong Kong people, but they cannot be tolerant about the declining of income from mainland China, so they

3　カナダは肝心なことを判断すべき

　ただ、カナダの人たちは「自分たちはアメリカではないが、アメリカの隣の国なので、ほぼ同じような傾向性である」と彼らに教えたいわけです。行きすぎた寛容さやリベラリズムばかりを考えたら、この国はたちまち弱くなってしまいます。アメリカのような強さではなく、弱さがあること、あるいは安易に強い国に追随しようとすることが、カナダの問題点ではないかと思います。

　これは日本の問題でもあります。私は幸福の科学グループの創始者兼総裁であり、私たちの政党もあります。日本の幸福実現党という名前です。日本では幸福実現党だけが、香港の自由のためにデモを行いました。ほとんどの日本人は傍観しているだけです。香港の人たちの悲劇は理解できるけれども、中国本土からの収入が減ることには耐えられないので、沈黙を守っているわけです。日本政府もそうですし、他の政党も一般国民もマスメディアもそうです。それが日本の状況です。

keep silence. Japanese government also, or other political parties also, and common people also, mass media also. That is the situation of Japan.

Even Canada sent a battleship near Hong Kong

Japan cannot live by their country only. Here, in Canada, you have more than 150 percent food supply and you have a lot of resources, so in some meaning, you are very strong to survive. But Japan is not so good at the capability of how to survive in the near future, so they cannot decide on pivotal things.

Even in Canada, Prime Minister Trudeau cannot decide on a lot, especially pivotal things, I mean, very difficult but important things which are problems all over the world. For example, Hong Kong problem. He sent one ship, battleship-type of ship, to the sea near Hong Kong. I've read, in Japan, about that.

カナダさえ香港近辺に軍艦を派遣

　日本は自国の力だけでは生きていくことができません。ここカナダでは、食料自給率が150パーセント以上ありますし、資源も豊富なので、ある意味で皆様は非常に生存能力が高いわけですが、日本は、「近い将来、どう生き延びていくか」という能力にあまり長けていないため、肝心なことについて判断することができないのです。

　カナダでも、トルドー首相は多くのことを判断できずにいます。特に、肝心な問題、非常に難しいけれども重要な、世界的問題になっていることに関してそうです。たとえば香港の問題もそうであり、私は日本で「彼が軍艦タイプの船を一隻、香港の近海に派遣した」というニュースを目にしました。それは良い判断ではあります

31

It's a good but curious decision. Even Trudeau sent military force. Oh, it's astonishing for Japanese people. He changed. Before the election, he changed a little.

4 What I Want to Say about Global Warming

Global warming has been the trend for the last 10,000 years

And another problem is, as you know, 16-year-old young lady, Ms. Greta Thunberg came to Canada and had a conversation with Mr. Trudeau for 15 minutes, and after that, Greta said, "Ah, you are going to do nothing!" He was scolded. He usually says, "I'm sorry." It's a Japanese way of thinking. So, yeah, indeed he's a good man, but he is indecisive.

が、奇妙な判断です。トルドー氏でさえ軍隊を送るとは、日本人には驚きです。彼は選挙を前にして少し変わったようです。

4　地球温暖化説について

温暖化は1万年前から続いている

　そしてもう一つの問題は、ご存じのとおり16歳の少女グレタ・トゥーンベリさんがカナダに来て、トルドー氏と15分間対談し、その後グレタさんは「何もしてくれないんですね！」と言い、彼は叱られてしまいました。彼は「すみません」と言ってばかりいますが、それは日本的な考え方です。彼は実際、良い方ではありますが、決断力に欠けると思います。首相ですから、グレタ・

4 What I Want to Say about Global Warming

I think so. He's a prime minister. He doesn't have any need to talk with Ms. Greta Thunberg. She said global warming is the death of this modern society, and she scolded a lot of adults all over the world.

But I want to say that, she finally usually says, "It's a science. Obey science. Science is everything," like that. But I am older than her, so I've learned a lot. And now, I'm a spiritual master, so I know this 10,000 years' history of the people. I must say that Ice Age ended about 10,000 years ago, and then global warming has been keeping its trend and this Earth became warmer and warmer. It led to a lot of civilizations to flourish. She usually says that the emission of CO_2 is bad and carbon dioxide is harmful to humankind, but in the standpoint of science, it's not true.

Carbon dioxide—it means the plants of the Earth can absorb a lot of energy from the air and there can spread a lot of green in this world. It will feed

トゥーンベリさんと話さなければいけない必要性はない
わけですが、彼女は「地球温暖化はこの現代社会の死を
意味する」と言って世界中の多くの大人たちを叱っていま
す。

　ただ、私が言いたいのは、彼女は最後はいつも「それ
は科学です。科学に従ってください。科学がすべてです」
などと言っていますが、私は彼女より年上なので多くの
ことを学んできています。さらに、現在では霊的なマス
ターとなっておりますので、ここ１万年の人類の歴史を
知っています。言っておかなければならないのは、約１
万年前に氷河期が終わり、そこからずっと地球温暖化の
傾向が続いていて、地球が次第に温かくなってきたとい
うことです。そのおかげで数多くの文明が繁栄してきま
した。彼女はいつも「CO_2 の排出は悪いことで、二酸
化炭素は人類にとって有害である」と言っていますが、
それは科学的見地から言って正しくありません。

　二酸化炭素の意味としては、それによって地球上の植
物が空気中から多くのエネルギーを吸収することができ
き、この世界に豊かな緑を広げて動物たちを養うことが

animals in this world, and after that, a lot of people can live on this Earth. So, this has been the trend. Science can decide almost nothing about this one. And, I think the next age will be the beginning of the Ice Age, I mean the Glacial Age. So, you don't think too much about that.

Behind global warming theory lies communist thinking

This kind of opinion is environment-friendly and it is common in the Canadian people, I think, but this opinion just attacks President Donald Trump's policy. I think so. And behind this opinion, there is some kind of communist thinking. Indeed, there is a lot of activity. So, we can't think so simply about that.

So, I want to say to you that you can prosper more and have industrialization and more population. It's

でき、だからこそ多くの人間がこの地球上で生きることができるのです。こういう流れがあるわけで、科学がこれに関して決められることは、ほとんどありません。そして、次の時代は氷河期の始まりになると思いますが、これについて皆様はあまり考えていません。

温暖化説の背後にある共産主義的考え方

この種の意見は環境に優しいので、カナダでは一般的だと思いますが、この意見はドナルド・トランプ大統領の政策を攻撃しているだけであると思います。この意見の背後には、ある種の共産主義的な考え方があります。実際に、いろいろな活動がありますので、それについては、あまり単純に考えるわけにはいきません。

ですから私が申し上げたいのは、皆様はもっと繁栄することができ、工業化や人口増を進めることができると

4 What I Want to Say about Global Warming

not so bad. It's already considered in heaven. So, my opinion is not so major in the world, but please just think about that. It's not the science only. It's the limited science.

いうことです。それは決して悪いことではありません。すでに天上界で検討済みのことなのです。私の意見は世界の中ではあまりメジャーではありませんが、どうかそのように考えてください。科学だけでいいわけではありません。そういう科学には限界があるのです。

5 Real Responsibility Means World Justice

We must stop the poverty and war in the world

We just think about the more important thing. That is, for example, the poverty, how to solve the poverty of the world. Billions of people are suffering from poverty. How can we solve this problem? Please think about that. It's very important, and it's the mission of an advanced country, I think. Canada has the capacity to help the people of the poverty country, so you can produce more wealth to help them. I just want to say that, if "Trudeau" means "responsibility," its responsibility must be real responsibility to save the people of the world.

One is, stop the poverty of the world; another one is, stop the confusion or war of the world. We must engage in such kind of activities. You can, of

5　本当の「責任」とは 世界正義を担うこと

世界の貧困と戦争の問題に取り組むべき

　私たちが考えているのは、それよりもっと重要なことです。たとえば「貧困」です。世界の貧困を解決する方法です。数十億の人々が貧困に苦しんでいます。どうすればこの問題を解決できるのか。それについて考えてください。これは非常に重要なことであり、先進国の使命であると思います。カナダには貧困国の人々を助けるだけの力があります。皆様は、彼らを助けるためにもっと富を生み出すことができます。「トルドーという名が『責任』を意味するなら、その責任とは、世界の人々を救う本物の責任でなければならない」と申し上げたいと思います。

　一つは世界の貧困をなくすことであり、もう一つは世界から混乱や戦争をなくすことです。私たちは、そうした活動に取り組まねばなりません。それは当然、皆様にできることなのです。もちろん日本も、そういったこと

course. Of course, Japan should do like that. We have potential, but both countries haven't done enoughly.

Deciding nothing means no responsibilities, not tolerance

So, we must define the meaning of responsibility again. It's not "the peaceful way of living of your own nation" only. Responsibility means the world justice and what is the Truth of this Earth. I think so.

People of both sides will appear if you decide something. We know about that. But if you hesitate to decide, it only means not tolerance, but just floating over the global world. So you, Canadian people, must be one of the leaders of the world. You have such kind of power inside. Only a strong opinion is required. If you don't want to have any trouble and want to escape from any trouble, you can decide almost nothing, and it means no responsibilities. I think so.

をするべきです。私たちにはその潜在的な力があるのですが、両国とも十分にやれてはいません。

決断を避けるのは「寛容」ではなく「無責任」

　ですから、「責任」の意味を定義し直さなければなりません。それは、自国が平和的に生きていくことだけではありません。責任とは、「世界正義」であり、「地球的真理とは何か」という意味であると思います。

　何か物事を決めれば、賛否、両方の人々が出てきます。そのことはわかっていますが、判断を尻ごみしていては、それは寛容ではなく、ただ、グローバルな世界のなかを漂流しているに過ぎません。カナダの皆様も世界のリーダーにならなくてはいけません。皆様にはその力が備わっています。あと必要なのは、力強い意見です。「何も問題を起こしたくない、トラブルから逃げたい」ということであっては、ほとんど何の決断もできず、「無責任」になってしまうでしょう。

6 The Common Base of Prosperity of Taiwan and Hong Kong

China has not experienced real democracy

I made a lecture in Taiwan also, this March, and at that place, I said, "The prosperity of Taiwan is based on their freedom and it's precious to keep their peace and their prosperity and the happiness of the people. No one can destroy the situation." And I sometimes say to Xi Jinping that, "China has not experienced real democracy in its 5,000 years." They cannot understand what I want to say.

Xi Jinping's guardian spirit, in my books, usually says that he cannot understand the meaning of democracy and the meaning of freedom of politics, voting or like that. It just means confusion. In China, historically, they required one-China policy. They are seeking for one China, and the total country, they

6 台湾と香港の「繁栄」の基盤とは

中国は本物の民主主義を経験していない

　私は今年の３月に、台湾でも説法をしました。その際に、「台湾の繁栄は彼らの自由に基づいており、彼らの平和と繁栄と国民の幸福を維持するのが尊いことであり、その状態を壊すことは誰にもできない」と話しました。私は時おり習近平に、「中国はその五千年の歴史において、本物の民主主義を経験していない」と言っています。ですから、彼らは私の言わんとすることが理解できないわけです。

　習近平の守護霊は、私の著書の中でよく、「民主主義の意味や、投票の自由などの政治的自由の意味が、理解できない。それは混乱でしかない」と言っています。中国は歴史的に「一つの中国」政策を必要としてきました。彼らは一つの中国を目指しており、統一国家を求めてきたのです。彼らは本物の民主主義を経験していません。

wanted. They've not experienced real democracy, but in Hong Kong, there is.

The starting point of Umbrella Revolution and Hong Kong Revolution

I also made a lecture in Hong Kong in 2011. On the day of typhoon, there were more than 1,300 people there, and I asked them. They were thinking just to change their Hong Kong-like thinking to mainland China-like thinking, or escape from Hong Kong. They were thinking these two only. I indicated them, "There is a third way for you. Please change China through the prosperity of Hong Kong." This prosperity comes, one is from the faith to God, and one is from the freedom of the people—freedom of activity, freedom of thinking, freedom of expression, freedom of voting, and freedom of election, of course. These are the common base of prosperity.

しかし、香港にはそれがあります。

雨傘革命と香港革命の原点

　私は香港でも2011年に説法をしました。台風の日でしたが千三百人以上の人が集まり、私は彼らにお願いしました。香港の人たちは、自分たちの香港的な考え方を中国本土的な考え方に変えるか、さもなくば香港から逃げるか、この二つしか考えていませんでしたので、私は「第三の道があります。香港の繁栄を通して中国を変えてください」という考えを提示しました。その繁栄とは、一つには神への信仰から来るものであり、もう一つには人々の自由から来るものです。活動の自由、思想の自由、表現の自由、投票の自由、そしてもちろん選挙の自由です。これらが、「繁栄」の共通の基盤なのです。

I said to them, "So, Hong Kong people, you should be the teacher of next-age China. This is the third way." This was the first point for them, and three years later, there occurred the Umbrella Revolution in 2014. They were defeated at that time, but again, they made a demonstration, and now, I call it Hong Kong Revolution again.

私は彼らに、「香港のみなさん、あなたがたが次の時代の中国の教師となるべきです。これが第三の道です」と言いました。これが彼らにとって最初のポイントとなり、その三年後に雨傘革命が起きました。2014年です。その時は敗れましたが、彼らは再びデモを行い、今、私はそれを再び「香港革命」と呼んでいます。

7 China's Ethnic Suppression and Totalitarian Regime

Democracy and freedom will make China greater than as it is

I hope... Canada is between two powers, one is the democratic power, and another is the economic profit. China is intruding, but I dare say, I don't hate Chinese people. I like them. I love them. I want them to be happier. So, I ask them, "Why don't you experience democracy, or the freedom of speech or expression or voting?" It's one examination for them, but it will make them greater than as it is. It means they can be on the same ground to discuss with Western people. So, I ask them to do so.

This is the China problem, and China problem

7　中国の民族弾圧と全体主義体制

「民主」と「自由」が中国をより素晴らしくする

　私の願いはこうです。カナダは二つの力の狭間にあります。一つは「民主主義の力」であり、もう一つは「経済的利益」です。中国が侵入してきていますが、あえて申し上げます。私は中国の人たちが嫌いなわけではありません。彼らは好きです。彼らを愛しています。もっと幸福になっていただきたいと願っています。ですから、彼らにお願いします。「民主主義や言論の自由、表現の自由、投票の自由を経験してみてはいかがですか」と。それは彼らにとって、一つの試験ではありますが、それによって、今よりもっと素晴らしくなっていけるでしょう。すなわち、西側の人たちと共通の議論の場に立てるようになるわけです。そのことをお願いしたいと思います。

　これは中国の問題であり、中国の問題にはウイグル

51

includes the Uyghur problem, and of course, Tibet problem and Inner Mongolia problem. They are suppressed a lot, but they are not broadcasted. This is a totalitarian regime. I already said it in Taiwan, the meaning of totalitarian regime. There are three symbols. One is, there is a mass murder, or violence on many people. And the second is the existence of secret police. And the third is the concentration camp. These three are the characteristics of totalitarian system. It was shown by Adolf Hitler in Germany, and also, it was shown by Stalin in Soviet Russia.

Checkpoint: belief in God and fundamental rights

"Communism and capitalism" is not the real dividing indication. But just think about two things: one is, "Is there any belief in God or not?" another one is, "Is there any fundamental rights in there or not?" This is very, very important. I love Chinese people, but in

問題や、当然チベット問題や内モンゴルの問題も含まれます。彼らは激しい弾圧を受けていますが、それが報道されることはありません。これが全体主義体制です。それに関しては、すでに台湾で述べました。全体主義体制の意味です。それを象徴するものは三つあり、一つは、「大量殺戮あるいは多数に対する暴力」です。二つ目は「秘密警察の存在」であり、三つ目は「強制収容所」です。この三つが全体主義体制の特徴であり、ドイツのアドルフ・ヒットラーやソ連のスターリンの例が示すとおりです。

そこに「信仰」と「基本的人権」はあるか

それを見分けるための本当の指標は、「共産主義か資本主義か」ではありません。そうではなく、次の二点だけを考えてください。一つは「神への何らかの信仰があるかどうか」であり、もう一つは「そこに基本的人権があるかどうか」です。ここが、きわめて重要です。私は

7 China's Ethnic Suppression and Totalitarian Regime

this regime, formally, Xi Jinping denies the faith or the importance of faith. And also, they don't believe in communism. They are really using capitalism, especially in south part of China. They are just using communism by the Machiavellism-like meaning.

中国の人々を愛していますが、彼らの政治体制では公式には、習近平は信仰や信仰の大切さを否定しています。そして、彼らは共産主義も信じてはいません。彼らは実際には、特に中国の南部では資本主義をとっていて、共産主義のほうは単にマキャベリズム的な意味合いで使っているだけです。

8 God is Not Dead

So, it's time to change, I think. World is required to change. More than one billion people are under the control of one policy or one person; this is apt to collapse the freedom and prosperity and faith of this Earth.

So, please teach the good things from Canada to such kind of countries. I think so. Especially, this country is, more than 75 percent are Christian, I've heard so. But in reality, there is no God in Canada because you have short history, so no one can consider more than 500 years ago. Just, you can imagine, "Two thousand years ago, there used to be Jesus Christ, but it's very far away from here. We don't know. Who is God, we don't know." This is a reality.

8 神は死んでいない

　ですから、今こそ変えるべき時であると思います。世界は変化を求められています。十億人以上の人々が、一つの政策や一人の人間の支配下にあるというのは、この地球の「自由」と「繁栄」と「信仰」を崩壊させてしまいかねません。

　ですから、カナダからそういった国に、良いものを教えてあげていただきたいと思います。特に、この国では75パーセント以上の人がキリスト教徒であると聞いています。ところが、実はカナダには神がいません。歴史が浅いためです。五百年以上前のことに思い至ることのできる人がいません。ただ、「二千年前にはイエス・キリストがいたけれど、ここからはすごく遠い場所だし、わからない。神様とは誰なのか、わからない」と想像するしかないのが実情です。

8 God is Not Dead

So, I want to say that

God is alive.

God is not dead.

God is watching you.

God is leading you.

God wants to save you,

Save such people who are suffering in this world

By dint of evil spirits or evil thinking

Or devil-like thinking.

God is fighting.

God has been fighting, even now.

So, please remake your religion

into a stronger one.

It is your responsibility, I think.

8　神は死んでいない

ですから、私は申し上げたいのです。

神は生きています。

神は死んではいません。

神はあなたがたを見守っています。

神はあなたがたを導いています。

神はあなたがたを救いたいと願っています。

この世界にあって、悪霊や悪しき考え方、

悪魔的な考え方のために

苦しんでいる人々を救いたいのです。

神は戦っています。

神は今もなお、戦っているのです。

ですから、あなたがたの宗教を

もっと力強いものにつくり変えていってください。

それこそが、あなたがたの「責任」であると思います。

9 After Visiting the Gay Town in Toronto

A lost spirit appeared in my hotel room

And I have another idea regarding you. I visited the gay town, it's famous, especially in Toronto. And in this meaning, you are the leading country of the world. It is the appearance of tolerance or diversity or belief in the variety of the possibility.

But... I've been to gay town and saw the statue of Alexander Wood*, and I took a picture with the statue, but after that, I went back to the hotel and there appeared Alexander Wood. And he said to me, "I am the God. I am the new God of the future." But I asked him, "Where are you now?" He said he is living in gay town now. This means he cannot understand the real aspect of another world, where is

---

* Alexander Wood (1772 – 1844) was the pioneer of the Gay Village in Toronto, Canada where homosexual people gather. The author had recorded "Spiritual Interview with Alexander Wood" on October 3 (Canada time), just three days before this lecture.

9　トロントのゲイタウンを訪れて

ホテルにやってきた「迷える霊」

　そして、皆様に関して、もう一つ私が考えていることがあります。私はゲイタウンを訪れました。特にトロントでは有名な場所です。この問題に関して、皆様の国は世界をリードしています。それは、寛容さや、多様性や、様々な可能性を信じるという考え方の現れではあります。

　しかし、私はゲイタウンに行き、アレキサンダー・ウッド（注）の像を見て、その像と並んで写真を撮ってからホテルに帰ったところ、アレキサンダー・ウッドが出てきました。彼は「私は神である。未来の新しい神である」と言っていましたが、「あなたは今どこにいるのか」と聞いてみると、「ゲイタウンにいる」と答えました。これは、彼があの世の実相について、どこが天国でどこが地獄なのか、わかっていないことを意味しています。そ

(注) **アレキサンダー・ウッド(1772〜1844)**　カナダ・トロントにあるゲイの人々が集まるエリア、通称ゲイヴィレッジの創設者。著者は本講演の3日前、カナダ時間10月3日に「アレキサンダー・ウッドの霊言」を収録した。

heaven and where is hell. He cannot understand. But he thinks that he is the God of new age.

LGBT matter in Christian and Japanese societies

So, this is just the pointing out of the problem. If you want to know a lot regarding this matter, please come to our branch office. I have a lecture already recorded. But now, I don't want to say anymore about this problem. This is a Canadian problem, but it's more than that; it's the Christian society's problem.

Japan is not a Christian society, but Japan is also aiming to change our constitution. Our Japanese constitution says that both male and female can marry, so Japan is just thinking about the amendment of constitution, but it's very difficult now, so they made laws only. Some cities set up that kind of law and people can make same-sex marriage in several cities in Japan, but it's not the total tendency.

れすらわからないのに、自分は新時代の神だと思っているわけです。

キリスト教社会と日本に広がるLGBT問題

　この場では、問題点を指摘するだけにとどめておきます。この件について詳しく知りたい方は、私たちの支部にいらしてください。すでに、これに関する説法を収録してありますが、今はこの問題についてこれ以上お話ししようとは思いません。これはカナダの問題ですが、それを超えて、キリスト教社会の問題です。

　日本はキリスト教社会ではありませんが、日本も憲法を変えようとしています。日本国憲法には「結婚できるのは男性と女性の両性である」と書かれていますので、日本はまさに憲法の修正を考えています。しかし、それは現時点ではきわめて難しいため、法律を作っているだけです。そうした法律を作って同性婚ができるようにしている日本の都市もありますが、それが全体的傾向になってはおりません。

10 The Reason We Are Here

The human soul is made of a group of souls

But I want to say, this is "the reason we are here."
We are not a material being, a material existence
only. God created human souls. It was a very ancient
age. And after that, some space people, outer space
people, joined in our earthly living. It's written in
The Laws of the Sun, as you have seen before this
lecture. It's very difficult and confusing, but we have
more than hundreds of millions of years' experience

１０ 「私たちがここにいる理由」

人間の魂はグループを作っている

　しかし、私が申し上げたいのは、それこそが「私たちがここにいる理由」であるということです。私たちは単なる物質的なもの、物質的存在ではありません。神が人間の魂を創ったのです。はるかなる古い時代のことです。その後、いくつかの宇宙人、地球外の人々が、私たち地球人の生活に加わってきました。そのことは、この説法の前にご覧になったとおり、『太陽の法』に書かれています。非常に難しく、わかりづらくはありますが、私た

 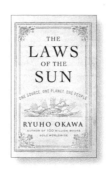

『太陽の法』（幸福の科学出版刊）とその英訳版 *The Laws of the Sun*
(New York: IRH Press, 2018)
The Japanese and English versions of *The Laws of the Sun*.

in this Earth living as a human being.

So, this is a weak point of Christianity. I must say that we, human beings, have souls before we are born into this world. We have past lives. Christians sometimes say that it's an evil thinking, but it's true. I examined more than 900 times and published more than 500 books about that. We have past lives. And one of them... I mean, we are a group. You heard that, "soulmate" or "soul brothers"-like words already. Yes, indeed. We have not one energy in us. We have several souls in our own group. One of them is born into this world, into this body, and grows up and goes back to heaven. This is the real explanation.

ちには何億年もの間、この地球上で人間として生きてき
た経験があるのです。

　ですから、ここがキリスト教の弱点です。「私たち人
間には、この世に生まれてくる前にも魂があるのだ」と
いうことをお伝えしなければなりません。私たちには過
去世があります。キリスト教では、これは悪しき考え方
だと言われることがありますが、真実です。私はそのこ
とを九百回以上も調査し、それについての本を五百冊以
上、出してきました。私たちには過去世があります。そ
のうちの一つが――つまり、私たちはグループを作っ
ているのです。「ソウルメイト」とか「魂のきょうだい」
といった言葉をお聞きになったことがあるでしょう。そ
うなのです。私たちの中にはエネルギーが一つしかない
わけではありません。いくつかの魂からなるグループで
あって、そのなかの一人がこの世に生まれ、この肉体に
宿り、成長し、天国に還っていくのです。これが正しい
説明です。

The human soul can be born as male or female

So, at first, God created both male and female, but our teachings show that the human soul can be born as male or female. Both are choiceable. You can choose both sides. When you are born as a man or when you are born as a woman, it means, during your lifetime in this world, several decades, you can acquire new character. And your new character, I mean, what you are, can be kept to the next reincarnation. This is the reality of spiritual aspect.

人は男女どちらに生まれることもできる

　神は初めに、男性と女性の両方を創りました。しかし、私たちの教えによれば、人間の魂は男性として生まれることも女性として生まれることもできます。両方とも選択可能です。どちらを選ぶこともできるのです。そして、男性あるいは女性として生まれたなら、それは、この世に生きている数十年の間に新しい個性を獲得することができることを意味します。「その新しい個性が、次の転生まで、あなたの姿として保たれる」というのが、霊的な実相です。

11 In This Materialistic World, Be Spiritual

So, we came here to experience a new age, a modern society, and make new character and go back to another world. Some become new angels through the education of this three-dimensional world, and some make mistakes and go down to hell. But it is also an experience. Hell is a hospital for them. They don't know clearly about their spirituality in their lives, so they are going to a hospital in the spiritual world. And after they awaken, they can go back to heaven.

So, all is teaching us
That the most important thing
Is to learn how to live in this world,
In your materialistic body.

１１　物質世界にあって霊的に生きる

　私たちが今ここに来ているのは、新たな時代を、現代社会を経験し、新しい個性を形づくって、あの世に還るためです。この三次元における教育を通して、新たに天使となる人もいます。なかには、間違いを犯して地獄に堕ちる人もいますが、それもまた「経験」なのです。地獄は彼らにとって病院です。彼らは生前、自分の霊的本質についてはっきりわかっていないので、霊界の病院に行き、目覚めを得たのちに天国に還ることができるのです。

　ですから、この世において物質的な肉体を持ちながら、
　いかに生きるべきかを学ぶのが
　いちばん大切なことであり、
　すべては、それを私たちに教えてくれているのです。

11 In This Materialistic World, Be Spiritual

But how you can realize

What you are and what you should do

Will decide your afterlife.

It's God's rule.

God does not divide or sentence you.

You, yourself, decide your destiny.

This is the reason

We are living in this world,

In Canada, in the United States,

Brazil, or Uganda, or other country

Who are watching my lecture now.

This is the reason. This world is materialistic, but in this materialistic world, be spiritual. That's the main reason of this life. Thank you very much.

11 物質世界にあって霊的に生きる

しかし、「自分とは何であり、何をなすべきか」を
いかに悟ることができるか。
それによって、あなたの来世が決まります。
それが神の法則です。
神があなたがたを分けたり
判決を下したりするのではありません。
あなた自身が自分の運命を決めるのです。

これが、私たちがカナダ、アメリカ、
ブラジル、ウガンダその他、
いま私の説法を観ている他の国々で、
この世界で生きている理由なのです。

　これが理由です。この世は物質的な世界ですが、この
物質世界において、霊的であってください。それこそが、
この人生の主たる理由です。ありがとうございました。

第 2 章

Q&A Session
（質疑応答）

October 6, 2019 at The Westin Harbour Castle, Toronto, Canada
（2019年10月6日　カナダ・トロント、ザ・ウェスティン・ハーバー・キャッスルにて）

1 New Faith to Spread in North America

Q1 I would appreciate your advice about building Toronto Shoshinkan. Please come back to Canada again.

Canada has a lot of hidden power

Ryuho Okawa If I'll come to Canada next time, I want to use, instead of Air Canada, JAL or ANA, or like that. It's not so comfortable. I couldn't sleep even a minute. It might be the second time for me, even one minute I couldn't sleep. So, it means, not so many businessmen or important people come to Canada, and only sightseeing people come to Canada. I think so.

Indeed, Japanese people should know a lot about Canada, be more concerned about Canada. If we took survey in Japan, "Who is the prime minister of Canada?" less than 50 percent can answer that

1　北米に広めるべき新たな信仰とは

質問1　トロント正心館を建立するためのアドバイスを
いただければ幸いです。そして、またぜひカナダにお越
しください。

カナダは大きな力を秘めている

大川隆法　次にカナダに来るとしたら、エア・カナダの
代わりにJALかANAなどを使いたいと思います。あ
まり快適ではなく、1分も眠れませんでした。1分も眠
れなかったというのは二度目かと思います。ビジネスマ
ンや重要人物はあまりカナダに来ておらず、観光客しか
カナダに来ていないのではないかと思います。

　実際、日本人はもっとカナダについて知り、カナダに
関心を持たなければいけません。日本で「カナダの首相
は誰ですか」とアンケートを取れば、その質問に答えら
れる人は50パーセント以下です。ただ、カナダは大き

question. But Canada has a lot of capacity, I think, and Canada has a lot of hidden *daikokutens*. I think so. They are supporters for Happy Science.

Japanese people usually think "foreigner" means the people of the United States, but it's not enough, of course. Please teach what Canadians think about, and do something characteristic to other countries. You can do more than that.

Indeed, we need more members in Canada. This is another answer to, "The Reason We Are Here." "To become members of Happy Science," another answer is this one. Or, the reason we are here, "Because we want to be daikokutens."

Happy Science accepts believers of other religions

We are very tolerant. We are accepting people who are believers in other religions, for example, Islamic

な力を持っていると思いますし、カナダには数多くの隠れた大黒天がいると思います。大黒天とは幸福の科学を支える方たちのことです。

日本人は、普通は外国人と言えばアメリカ人のことだと思っていますが、それはもちろん十分ではありません。ぜひ、カナダの人たちが考えていることを教えてください。そして、他国に向けて、何か特徴的なことをしてください。皆様には、それ以上のことができると思います。

実際、カナダにはもっと多くの信者が必要です。それが、「私たちがここにいる理由」の、もう一つの答えです。「幸福の科学の信者になるため」、もう一つの答えはこれです。あるいは、私たちがここにいる理由は「大黒天になりたいから」です。

幸福の科学は他宗の信者も受け入れている

私たちは非常に寛容で、他の宗教の信者である方も受け入れています。たとえばイスラム教徒、キリスト教徒、

79

1 New Faith to Spread in North America

people or Christian people, Buddhist people or Japanese Shinto people. There are a lot of members who have such kind of belief in them because we are combined, and the founders of those religions were—at that time, almost all of the worldwide religions were taught by me from the heavenly world, so I know a lot about them. They are not different. We are seeking for the same direction, just save people and just want to make people happier. This is the "common ground" for us. So, believe in Happy Science.

In Japan, we have a lot of followers, for example, other political parties' members or other religious members. For example, in Japan, there's Jodo Shinshu, Shinran's teaching's followers. It has 10 million members, they say, but its top is our member. So, we have a lot of members outside of Happy Science, for example. And in India, we have a lot of members. We don't have enough branches, of course.

80

仏教徒、日本神道の信者などです。それらの信仰を持っている当会の信者はたくさんいます。なぜなら、私たちの宗教ではそれらが統合されていますし、それらの宗教の開祖は――当時、ほとんどの世界宗教は天上界から私の教えを受けていたので、私は彼らのことをよく知っているのです。それらは別のものではありません。私たちが求める方向は同じです。ただただ人を救いたい、人々をもっと幸福にしたいだけです。それが私たちの「コモン・グラウンド」（共通の土台）です。ですから、幸福の科学を信じてください。

　日本には私たちの信者が大勢います。他の政党にもいますし、他の宗教の信者にもいます。たとえば、日本には浄土真宗があります。親鸞の教えを信じる人たちで、信者は一千万人いると言われていますが、そこのトップの方は私たちの信者です。ですから、幸福の科学の外側にも多くの信者がいるわけです。インドにも信者が大勢いて、もちろん支部が足りていません。

1 New Faith to Spread in North America

So, next stage is how to manage worldwide activities through breeding the leaders, and of course, thinking about the business mind-like thinking. Each leader must have such kind of thinking. I, myself, was, during my younger age, my twenties, a member of a trading house, and I worked on Wall Street. I can imagine a lot of branches all over the world, and can manage them. So, I know, and I have dreams of such kind.

Please ask our lecturers to attract a lot of people, more than as it is. If I go to Africa, there come more than tens of thousands of people. When I went to Uganda, there came three broadcasting companies including one national company. They broadcast my lecture, and more than 30 million people watched it. In Nepal, also the same; in India, also the same; and in Sri Lanka, also the same. It is a Buddhist country, so they came to see me.

ですから次の段階は、リーダーの養成やビジネス・マインド的な思考を持つことを通して、いかに世界的活動を運営していくかです。リーダーの一人ひとりが、そうした考え方を持たなければいけません。私自身も若い頃、20代は商社マンとしてウォール街で働いていましたので、世界中に多くの支部があるのをイメージできますし、それらを運営することもできます。ですから知識もあり、そうした夢もあるわけです。

ぜひ、今よりもっと多くの人を惹きつけるよう、当会の講師に頼んでください。私がアフリカに行けば何万人もの人が集まります。ウガンダにも行きましたが、そこでは国営放送一社を含む三社の放送局が来てテレビで中継され、三千万人以上の人が私の説法を観ました。ネパールでも同じですし、インドも、スリランカも同じです。仏教国なので私に会いに来たのです。

God Thoth governs North America

But in Christian society, Western society, people already belong to churches, so they don't want to come on Sunday. But please teach them: I am a teacher of Jesus Christ. This was true, and this is true, now. So, please tell them. This is El Cantare, the meaning of El Cantare, meaning of Elohim, Allah, or ancient age God.

And, in this area, north part of the American continent, you have God. Its name is Thoth. Yeah, you have. Thoth is one of the soul brothers of El Cantare. He is the Almighty God of Atlantis age. He is. He is governing the spiritual world of Canada and the United States. So, you can believe in God. He is, and He is connected to me.

So, it's a new faith, but please spread these teachings. We need more members, I ask you. I want to save people who are suffering now. So, we need a

北米を司る神「トス」の存在

　ただ、西洋のキリスト教社会の人たちは、すでに教会に属しているので、日曜には来たがりませんが、ぜひ、私がイエス・キリストの先生であることを教えてあげてください。それが真実だったのであり、今も真実ですので、どうか伝えてください。これがエル・カンターレであり、エル・カンターレの意味であり、エローヒムやアッラーや古代の神の意味なのです。

　そして、この北米大陸の地において、あなたがたにも神がいます。その神の名を「トス」と言います。そう、神がいるのです。トスはエル・カンターレの魂の兄弟の一人であり、アトランティス時代の全知全能の神です。この神が存在しており、カナダとアメリカの霊界を司っています。ですから、あなたがたは神を信じることができます。神が存在しており、私とつながっているのです。

　これは新しい信仰ですが、どうかこの教えを広めてください。私たちにはもっと仲間が必要ですので、お願いします。私は、現在苦しんでいる人たちを救いたいので

lot of members and we need a lot of people who are influenced by our teachings, of course.

I will do my best. We have millions of followers all over the world outside of Japan, but main point is, the people of the world are not so wealthy. Some people have less than one percent of the income of the Japanese people. This is the difficulty of activities. So, please cooperate. I will think with you.

す。ですから多くの仲間が必要ですし、多くの人たちに私たちの教えの影響を受けてもらうことも、やはり必要です。

　私も全力を尽くします。日本以外にも信じる人たちは何百万人もいますが、最大の問題は、世界の人たちはそれほど裕福ではないということです。日本人の収入の1パーセントに満たない人たちもいます。ここが活動の難しさなので、ご協力をお願いします。私も一緒に考えていきたいと思います。

2 Helping Patients Who Suffer from Drug Abuse

Q2 I'm working at a hospital, as a registered nurse in Los Angeles, right now. I have so many people suffering from drug abuse, and I think this is a big problem in the United States and, I believe, in Canada too. Many people, like young age, 20 or 30 years old, they are not compliant, they don't care about their life. And we try to teach the truth of the soul, but their cap is like a big rock, so they don't understand what we are saying.

So, I just want to know how to help them, how to give them the Truth. Yeah, so that's my main concern. Every time, when I take care of the patient, they don't listen to us, nothing. They come back and forth, to and from the hospital, because they want to do drugs. Many people are suffering, and

2　薬物乱用患者を救うには

質問2　私は現在、ロサンゼルスの病院で正看護師として働いておりますが、薬物乱用で苦しんでいる人が大勢います。これはアメリカでは大きな問題ですし、カナダでもそうだと思います。20歳から30歳くらいの若い人などの多くが社会のルールを遵守せず、自分の人生を大切にしていません。私たちが魂の真実を教えようとしても、大きな岩のようなもので頭にフタをされていて話が通じません。

　彼らを助けて真理を伝えるにはどうすればいいかを知りたいのです。それが何より心配なのです。毎回、患者のお世話をしてもまったく言うことを聞いてくれませんし、麻薬がほしくて病院を出たり入ったりしています。たくさんの人が苦しんでいて、そのために国力が大きく損なわれているのです。若い人が皆、それ

the country is losing much power because of that, because of the young-aged people all involved. So, I just want to know how to cope with this problem, in this country, and also in Japan too.

Pray for the power from heaven

Ryuho Okawa OK. Every country has its problem. Younger people have also problems and disease in heart. Yeah, it's very difficult to teach one by one because they acquired a lot of teachings for her or for him, or at his age or at her age, and thinking of parents has very much influence on them.

So, please meditate and pray for our heavenly guiding spirits. "Give me power to teach them. Give me power to persuade them. Give me power to save them." They will 100 percent assist you. There comes light of the stream, and it will give you super

に巻き込まれているからです。この国でそして日本で、この問題にどう対処すれば良いか、ご教示いただきたく存じます。

天上界の力を求めよ

大川隆法　わかりました。どの国にもそれぞれ問題があります。若い人たちも問題や心の病をかかえています。そう、一人ひとりに教えるのは実に難しいことです。その人に、その年齢なりに、いろいろな教えが入っていて、両親の考え方の影響もそうとう大きいからです。

　ですから、ぜひ瞑想をして、天上界にいる私たちの指導霊に祈ってください。「彼らを導く力をお与えください。彼らを説得する力をお与えください。彼らを救う力をお与えください」と祈ってください。100パーセント力を貸してくれます。光が流れ入り、その光によって偉

power, supernatural power to save people. Your words are not your words. They come from heavenly existence, through your throat, through your mouth. You can teach them. At that time, at that situation, at the individual, for what he needs, you can speak to a T. You can, yes.

Just pray for the souls of angels or bodhisattva, nyorai of Happy Science. There are more than 500 great angels and angels in heaven, for our group. So, you can. You can receive their power, spiritual power, and you can do everything through them. Even the bad-thinking people can change into good-thinking people. Or, even people who are suffering from going more than point of no return, I mean, who are destined to die, you can call them back to this world and give them new lives.

Our next movie describes about that. So, please ask other people to watch *Immortal Hero*. In it, I

大な力が、超自然的な救いの力が与えられます。言葉が自分の言葉ではなくなります。あなたの喉を、口を通して、天上界の存在から言葉が降りてきます。彼らを教えることができます。その「時」と「場合」と「人」に応じて相手に必要な、ぴったりの言葉を話すことができます。そう、できるのです。

幸福の科学の天使や菩薩、如来の魂に、ただただ祈ってください。天上界には私たちの指導霊団として、五百人以上の大天使や天使がいます。ですから、できます。彼らの力、霊的な力を受けることができます。そして、彼らを通してどんなことでもできるのです。悪いことを考えている人が良い考えに変わることもできますし、引き返せない段階を通り越して苦しんでいる人、つまり、死が確定したような人であっても、この世に呼び戻して新しい命を与えることができます。

これは私たちの次の映画で描かれていることです。ですから、ぜひ「世界から希望が消えたなら。」を観るこ

2 Helping Patients Who Suffer from Drug Abuse

answer a lot regarding your question. So, my answer is, "Require the power from heaven." You can be stronger. That's the conclusion.

2　薬物乱用患者を救うには

とをお勧めしてください。そのなかに、ご質問に関する答えをたくさん入れてあります。ですからお答えとしては、「天上界の力を求めてください」ということです。あなたはもっと強くなれます。それが結論です。

映画「世界から希望が消えたなら。」(製作総指揮・原案 大川隆法／ 2019 年 10 月 18 日日米加同時公開)
The movie, *Immortal Hero* (executive producer and original story by Ryuho Okawa, released simultaneously on October 18, 2019 in Japan, the U.S., and Canada).

3 The Real Meaning of Golden Age

Q3 My question to you today is regarding the Golden Age that you spoke of in your book, *The Laws of the Sun*. You said that the Golden Age will be dawning in the year of 2020. I would like to know more in depth, what is the Golden Age, and what mindset must the countries of the world have to make sure the Golden Age is the most powerful success.

Ryuho Okawa OK. The real meaning of the Golden Age. It will begin from 2020, I already said. It means, we will destroy atheists or non-believers in God on this Earth, and such kind of great power will be ruined from 2020 to 2030. For example, it means the gigantic country who doesn't believe in God and is just one-party system and communism-only country, will be destroyed by dint of God's power [*audience applauds*].

3 「ゴールデン・エイジ」の本当の意味とは

質問3　ご著書の『太陽の法』でおっしゃっていたゴールデン・エイジについてお尋ねします。2020年がゴールデン・エイジの夜明けだと言われていますが、ゴールデン・エイジとは何か、ゴールデン・エイジを最大限成功させるために世界の国々はどのようなマインドセットを持たなければいけないかについて、もっと深く知りたいと思います。

大川隆法　わかりました。ゴールデン・エイジの本当の意味ということですが、それは2020年から始まると、すでにお話ししています。それは、この地球上から無神論者や神への信仰を持たない人々を一掃し、2020年から2030年にかけて、そうした大きな力が滅んでいくということです。それはたとえば、神を信じない一党独裁、共産主義独裁の巨大な国家が、神の力によって倒されるということです（会場拍手）。

3 The Real Meaning of Golden Age

And, another answer is, there are people who are living miserably in this world, for example, poverty, and another one is under the war situation. They cannot live actively and happily. We will stop such kind of situation and make peace in this world. It's Buddha Land Utopia. It's a meaning of Golden Age. OK?

And, *you* are the expected person, one of expected people for that. So, I will do my best, but it's not my limit or our limit. We have a lot of members who have hidden powers within them. So, we make our powers together! Together our power, do great things on this Earth! Is it OK? [*Audience applauds.*]

OK. Thank you. See you again.

3 「ゴールデン・エイジ」の本当の意味とは

　もう一つの答えは、この世界には悲惨な人生を生きている人たちがいます。たとえば貧困であり、もう一つが戦時下の状況です。彼らは元気で幸福な人生を生きることができずにいます。私たちはそうした状況を終わらせ、世界に平和をもたらします。それが「仏国土ユートピア」であり、「ゴールデン・エイジ」の意味です。よろしいでしょうか。

　そして、あなたも、それを期待されています、期待されている一人です。ですから、私も全力を尽くしますが、私の、私たちの力はそれにとどまりません。私たちには内なる力を秘めたメンバーが数多くいます。私たちの力を合わせて、一体となった力で、この地上で偉大なる事業を成し遂げてください！ よろしいですか。（会場拍手）

　オーケー。ありがとうございました。またお会いしましょう。

第3章

Master Okawa's Answers to Canadian Activists
（カナダの活動家の質問に答える）

October 11, 2019 at Happy Science General Headquarters, Tokyo
（2019 年 10 月 11 日　東京、幸福の科学・総合本部にて）

This chapter is the transcript of the session recorded on October 11, 2019 at Happy Science General Headquarters. In the first part of the session, a video footage was shown; it was an on-site interview with three Canadian activists who attended the author's lecture, "The Reason We Are Here" on October 6 in Toronto, Canada. Then, two interviewers offered more detailed information on them, and the author gave his reply to each activist.

Activists

Gloria Fung, Canada-Hong Kong Link, President

Sheng Xue,
Vice President, The Federation for a Democratic China
Vice President of Canadian Coalition Against Communism

Rukiye Turdush, Uyghur Canadian Society, Former President

Interviewers from Happy Science

Motohisa Fujii

Executive Director
Special Assistant to Religious Affairs Headquarters
Director General of International Politics Division

Mayumi Kobayashi

Manager of International Politics Division
Religious Affairs Headquarters

★ Interviewers are listed in the order that they appear in the transcript. Their professional titles represent their positions at the time of the interview.

本章は2019年10月11日、幸福の科学・総合本部で収録された。収録の冒頭、10月6日のカナダ・トロントにおける著者講演会「The Reason We Are Here」に参加したカナダの活動家三名に講演終了直後の会場でインタビューした映像を上映した。その後、二名の質問者が補足説明し、それらを受けて著者が話した内容である。

インタビューに登場した活動家（登場順）

グロリア・ファン氏　（カナダ – 香港リンク代表）

盛雪氏　（民主中国陣線副主席、カナダ反共連盟副主席）

ルキエ・トールダッシュ氏　（カナダ・ウイグル協会前代表）

質問者（幸福の科学）
藤井幹久（ふじいもとひさ）　（理事 兼 宗務本部特命担当国際政治局長）
小林真由美（こばやしまゆみ）（宗務本部国際政治局チーフ）

※質問順。役職は収録当時のもの。

1 Interviews with Three Activists

MC Now, Master Ryuho Okawa will give us a lecture entitled, "Master Okawa's Answers to Canadian Activists." On October 6, after Master's Toronto lecture, "The Reason We Are Here," the International Politics Division interviewed Canadian activists to hear their comments. They asked us some questions. So today, Master will give us answers to those questions. First, please watch the interview video.

[Video footage of on-site interviews after the Toronto lecture]

Gloria Fung I feel very honored to be invited here to listen to Master Okawa's very enlightening lecture today because it has covered a lot of important topics in life—the importance of the intangible values of peace, love, happiness, and more importantly, the importance of the pursuit of Truth in life.

1　活動家３人のインタビュー

司会　それでは、大川隆法総裁先生より御法話「大川総裁、カナダの活動家の質問に答える」を賜ります。10月6日に、総裁先生のトロント御法話「私たちがここにいる理由」の終了後、国際政治局がカナダの活動家の方たちにインタビューし、コメントをいただきました。彼らからいくつか質問がありましたので、本日は総裁先生がそれらの質問にお答えくださいます。最初にインタビュー映像をご覧ください。

【以下、トロント講演　本会場でのインタビュー映像】

グロリア・ファン　本日は大川総裁先生のご法話にお招きいただき、まことに光栄に存じます。ご法話にはたいへん啓発されました。「平和」や「愛」や「幸福」などの目には見えない価値の大切さなど、人生で大切な論点について幅広く触れておられましたし、さらに大切なこととして、人生における「真理の探究」の大切さについ

I'm also enlightened by his call for concern for people around the world in their struggle against totalitarianism. This is particularly important for people like myself, who was originally from Hong Kong, because the Hong Kong people are now at the very forefront of battlefield in China fighting for core values of human rights, freedom, rule of law, and democracy, which we Canadians as well as people around the world cherish dearly. So, this is not just about Hong Kong, it's also a Canadian and an international issue. I therefore concur with Master Okawa that all of us need to support the people of Hong Kong.

I would like to seek his advice as what the people of Canada and the international community could do to support the Hongkongers in their fight against totalitarian suppression from the Chinese Communist Party, how we can stay united and take concrete

てもお話しくださいました。

　そしてやはり、世界中で全体主義に対して戦っている人々への関心を呼びかけてくださったことに啓発されました。私のように香港出身の人間にとって、この点は特に重要です。香港市民は今、中国の最前線で、人権や自由や法の秩序や民主主義といった核となる価値観のために戦っています。私たちカナダ人をはじめ世界中の人々もそれらの価値観を大切にしています。ですから、これは香港だけの問題ではなくカナダの問題でもありますし、国際的な問題なのです。ですから、すべての人が香港市民を支援する必要があるという点で、大川総裁に同感です。

　中国共産党の全体主義的圧政と戦っている香港人を支援するためにカナダの人々と国際社会は何ができるのか、また、世界に前向きな変化をもたらすために私たちが一致団結を続けて具体的行動を起こすにはどうすればいいのか、ご教示いただければ幸いです。

actions to make a positive change in this world.

Sheng Xue I feel very honored to be here, and I'd like to say thank you to Master because he brought the very important message to Canada in his first lecture here. He also mentioned that China needs to be changed.

Happiness is the most important thing to every individual. I truly believe so. That's why we are having our life and come to this world. Everybody is trying to look for happiness, but only people who have freedom, human rights and democracy can truly enjoy happy lives. So, the whole world won't enjoy freedom and happiness until the 1.4 billion people in China are liberated from fear under the tyranny. This is a great task and a very important thing for everybody to think about. And Master has the ability so I would like to know his plan to help people in China to enjoy happiness one day, without fear and

盛雪　参加させていただき、たいへん光栄です。総裁先生に感謝申し上げます。当地初のご法話で、カナダにとってたいへん重要なメッセージをいただきましたし、中国は変わる必要があるとも言及してくださいました。

　幸福は人間にとっていちばん大切なものだと、私は心から信じています。そのためにこそ私たちは生きていますし、この世に生まれてくるのです。誰もが幸福を探そうとしているわけですけれども、自由や人権や民主主義があってこそ、人は本当の意味で幸福な人生を享受することができます。ですから、14億の中国人が専制政治の恐怖から解放されないうちは、全世界が自由と幸福を享受することはありません。これはたいへんな仕事ですし、すべての人が考えなければならないきわめて重要な問題です。そして、総裁先生はその力をお持ちですので、いつの日か中国の専制政治による恐怖や迫害がなくなり、中国の人たちが幸福を享受できるようにしていくため

persecution from the Chinese tyranny.

Japan is becoming a great country, and is a democratic torch in Asia. I think Japan has the ability and responsibility to do more, especially to lead Asia for freedom and democracy. So, my question to Master is, "How can Japan do better and do more?" As he mentioned, related to the emergency situations in Hong Kong, the Japanese government doesn't do anything now, nor do other political parties; only Happiness Realization Party takes action, right? So, I really admire that a spiritual leader also can give comments on the real problems that we are facing today.

We need to enjoy freedom and human rights together, and have democracy as a political system of the country. But our world is far from perfect. Many people are living under fear and persecution, so they cannot enjoy happiness. I'd like to really contribute my life for more and more people to live with dignity.

に、どのような計画がおありなのか、知りたく思います。

日本は大国になりつつあり、アジアにおける民主主義の松明（たいまつ）です。日本には、特にアジアを自由と民主主義へと導いていくために、もっと多くのことをするだけの能力がありますし、その責任もあると思います。総裁先生に質問したいのは、「日本がもっと多くのことをやっていくためには、どうすればいいか」ということです。ご法話のなかでも、「香港の非常事態に関して、日本政府も他の政党も何もしていない」と言及されました。幸福実現党だけが行動されているのですよね。精神的（霊的）リーダーである方が、私たちが現在直面している現実の問題についてもコメントしてくださることができるというのは、本当に素晴らしいことだと思います。

私たちは共に自由を享受し、共に人権を有し、共に国家の政治体制として民主主義を持つ必要がありますが、この世界は完璧にはほど遠い状況です。恐怖と迫害のなかで生きている人が数多くいて、彼らは幸福を味わうことができません。私は、尊厳を持って生きていける人がもっともっと増えていくために、自分の人生を捧げ尽く

I came from China, and I'm a Chinese-Canadian. That's why I do care more about people in China. I think this is the nature of human beings. Don't forget that there are 1.4 billion people in China. It's a huge amount of life there. They cannot enjoy freedom, human rights and democracy, which makes the world actually very dangerous. People there are being brainwashed and pressured, and are becoming the enemies of freedom. This is the urgent threat to the whole world. Everybody needs to take the responsibility to make a change, as Master said that China needs to be changed.

Rukiye Turdush Thank you very much for having me today. I feel so honored to participate in this event. This is my prestige. I am an Uyghur and immigrated to Canada 20 years ago and now I am the representative of Uyghurs.

したいと思っています。

　私は中国出身の中国系カナダ人なので、なおのこと中国の人たちが心配なのです。それは人間として当然のことであると思います。中国には14億の人々がいることを忘れないでください。ものすごい数の人命がそこにあるのです。中国人が自由も人権も民主主義も享受することができていないため、実際、世界は非常に危険な状況にあります。洗脳や圧力を受けることで、中国の人たちが「自由の敵」となっていっているからです。これは全世界にとってさし迫った脅威です。すべての人が、この状況を変えるために責任を果たす必要があります。総裁が「中国は変わる必要がある」とおっしゃったからです。

ルキエ・トールダッシュ　本日はお招きくださり、まことにありがとうございました。ご法話に参加することができてたいへん光栄であり、誇りに思います。私はウイグル人で、20年前にカナダに移住し、現在ウイグル人の代表をしております。

I have a message for Master Ryuho Okawa, because he knows that more than three million Uyghur people in East Turkistan are suffering in the Chinese concentration camps. The Chinese empire colonized East Turkistan in 1949 and Uyghur people are living in open prison now.

What China is doing today is not only against the people but also it is against God because people in concentration camps are forced not to believe in Islam, and only to praise Xi Jinping and Chinese Communist Party. And they force people to transform their identity into Han Chinese. This is against God's will. God created diversity of people, but China declares war against God right now.

I think your organization's mission is to steer the power of people to fight against such evil regime to make a better world for the humanity. And we are willing to cooperate with you and the Hong Kong people to fight against the evil regime of Chinese

大川隆法総裁先生にお伝えしたいことがあります。総裁は、東トルキスタンのウイグル人が300万人以上、中国の強制収容所で苦しんでいることをご存じだからです。中華帝国が1949年に東トルキスタンを植民地にして、ウイグル人は今、屋根のない刑務所のような世界のなかで生きています。

中国がやっていることは人々に対してだけでなく、神に対する反抗でもあります。強制収容所ではイスラム教を棄教し、習近平と中国共産党だけを崇め、自分のアイデンティティを漢民族としてのアイデンティティに変えるよう強制されます。これは神の心に反しています。神は、人間の多様性を創造されたのに、中国は今、神に対して宣戦布告をしているのです。

皆様の団体の使命は、こうした悪しき体制に対して戦い、人類にとってより良い世界をつくるために、人々の力を結集することだと思います。私たちは皆様や香港の人たちと協力して、中国共産党の悪しき体制や、世界のいかなる悪しき政府に対しても、戦っていきたいと思い

Communist Party, and against any evil governments in this world. As people living in Canada, a democratic and free country, it is our prestige and unique responsibility to use this freedom to fight against evil.

As a Canadian, I would like to work together with you and my people will work with you too. Thank you very much for everything you have done. Your organization is the only one strong organization that can steer the power of people in grass root level as well as in government level, and make sure the people in the governments who are in power to do the right things.

As Master Ryuho Okawa said, the roots of all religions are one. Islam believes in only one God, Allah, so there is no conflict with what Master said. The Jewish people believe in Elohim. Actually we say Elohim when we pray. We all have the same God. So, Elohim and Allah, and whatever the god's name may be, they are actually only one God. Whatever

ます。民主的で自由な国であるカナダに住む者として、この自由を使って悪と戦うことは、私たちに与えられた特権でもあり特別の責任でもあるのです。

　私はカナダ人として皆様と一緒にやっていきたいですし、私の仲間もご一緒することと思います。これまでしてくださったことに本当に感謝しております。草の根レベルでも政府レベルでも人々の力を結集し、政府の権力者たちに正しい行動をとらせるようにすることができる強力な団体は、皆様以外にありません。

　大川総裁が説かれたように、すべての宗教の根本は一つです。イスラム教は唯一神アッラーを信じていますので、総裁がおっしゃったことと何の矛盾もありません。ユダヤ人はエローヒムを信じていますが、実際に私たちも「エローヒム」と言って祈りますので、私たちの神は同じなのです。エローヒムでもアッラーでも、その神の名前が何であっても、実際には唯一神のことなのです。

Master said has nothing to conflict with Islam. I'm happy with that.

It is people who changed things because of their own interests. Now we have to go back to the Truth. Like Master said, we have to unite as one and together with the power of the Creator we can change the world.

I would like Master Ryuho Okawa to mention Uyghur crisis in his speeches and lectures. He can raise awareness on what evil countries and governments are doing. What they're doing to Uyghur people is the fact and evidence. Many people don't know about China. Some people even say, "The Chinese government is a good government. They are not like American superpower and not going to invade other countries." I hope Master Ryuho Okawa raises Chinese issues so that people can understand the true color of China. Actually, no other regime is more evil than China.

総裁が説かれたことで何一つイスラム教と対立するものはないので、うれしく思います。

　人間が、自分たちの利益のために物事を変えてしまったのです。今こそ真理に立ち帰らなくてはなりません。総裁が説かれたように、私たちは一つに結びつかなくてはなりませんし、創造主の力と一体となることで、世界を変えていけるのです。

　大川隆法総裁先生には、様々なご法話のなかでウイグルの危機に言及していただきたいと思います。総裁先生は、悪しき国や政府がやっていることを人々に気づかせることができます。彼らがウイグル人に対してやっていることが、事実であり証拠です。中国については知らない人が多く、「中国政府はいい政府だ。超大国アメリカとも違うし、他国を侵略したりしないだろう」と言う人さえいます。大川隆法総裁先生が中国問題を取り上げてくださることで、人々が中国の本性を理解してくれることを願っています。実際、中国以上に悪しき体制はありません。

2 Answer to Ms. Fung: Advice to Supporters of Hong Kong Democratic Protests

MC Now, we will like to have a Q&A session with Master Okawa.

Ryuho Okawa OK. Is there anything you want to ask?

Fujii Thank you for today. We'd like to ask you questions on behalf of three activists. Firstly, I will introduce their background and activities. And then, Ms. Kobayashi will add our relationship with the activists. Finally, she will ask you questions.

First person was a female activist, Ms. Gloria Fung, president of Canada-Hong Kong link. She is not just one of the most prominent activists in Canada, I believe she is the most famous and important activist

2 ファン氏への回答
——香港の民主化デモ勢力への
アドバイス

司会　それでは、大川隆法総裁先生より質疑応答を賜り
ます。

大川隆法　オーケー。何か聞きたいことはありますか。

藤井　本日はありがとうございます。三人の活動家に代
わって質問させていただきます。最初に私から彼らの経
歴と活動について紹介し、その後、小林さんから、私た
ちと活動家の関係について補足し、最後に彼女から総裁
先生に質問させていただきます。

　最初の方は女性活動家で「カナダ‐香港リンク」代表
のグロリア・ファンさんです。カナダの最も著名な活動
家の一人というだけでなく、カナダで中国の共産党体制
に反対する最も有名で重要な活動家であると思います。

in Canada against China's communist regime. And she is gathering e-petition, because now is the time for the federal election in Canada. She is engaging to raise awareness among Canadian politicians. Not only the Liberal Party and the Conservative Party, but all Canadian politicians should be aware of the Hong Kong issue. That's her mission now. We have relationship with her, so Ms. Kobayashi will explain about her.

Kobayashi I met her for the first time in this May in Taiwan. She was attending as a representative from Canada to an event, which was to commemorate June 4th Tiananmen massacre. She had a very inspiring speech. So, I wanted her to come to our event as well. And when I invited her, she was very happy to attend the event because at that time her focus was on the e-petition that Mr. Fujii just said, she wanted to use this e-petition to push for Hong Kong to become

現在カナダは総選挙の時期なので、彼女は今、オンライン署名を集めて、カナダの政治家たちに関心を高めてもらう活動をしています。自由党や保守党だけでなく、すべてのカナダの政治家は香港問題に意識を向けるべきであるというのが彼女の現在の使命です。私たちは彼女とつながりがありますので、小林さんから彼女についてご説明します。

小林　今年の５月に台湾で彼女と初めてお会いしました。６月４日天安門大虐殺の記念行事にカナダ代表として参加され、たいへん感動的なスピーチをされていたので、私たちの行事にも参加していただきたいと思ってご招待しました。彼女が現在、力を入れて取り組んでいるのは藤井さんが言われたようにオンライン署名活動であり、カナダの選挙の争点として香港問題を推進したいという考えをお持ちだったため、非常に喜んで参加してくださったのです。

Canadian federal election issue.

And I'd like to ask you a question on behalf of her. She was seeking for your advice on what Canadians as well as people around the world could do in order to support the Hong Kong people in the fight against dictatorial suppression.

China's strategy to change the opinion of the world

Ryuho Okawa OK. They are very brave, I think, and they have conviction in their activities. It's good for them. I feel... the first person is Ms. Gloria Fung? She has power in her, of course, spiritual power, I felt. And her conviction is very strong. What she said will lead a lot of Canadian Chinese people. I think so.

But even in Canada, there are two groups. Generally speaking, one is acting for supporting

彼女の代わりに質問させていただきます。彼女は総裁先生に、「カナダや世界の人々は、独裁的な圧政と戦う香港の人たちをサポートするために何ができるか」についてご教示いただきたいとのことでした。

世界の意見を変えようとする中国の戦略

大川隆法　わかりました。実に勇敢な方たちだと思いますし、自分たちの活動に信念を持たれていますので、それは彼らとしては良いことだと思います。私の感じでは……一人目の方はグロリア・ファンさんですか。この方には内なるパワーがありますね。もちろん霊的パワーです。それを感じました。非常に信念の強い方であり、彼女の言葉は多くの中国系カナダ人を導いていくと思います。

ただ、カナダの中にも二つのグループがあります。大きく言って、一つは「香港を支持するために行動する人

Hong Kong, and another one is people who are protecting Beijing, China, including a lot of students from China. So, the Chinese society in Canada is not one. And I guess the number of the people who are living in Canada from mainland China is more than Hong Kong supporters. This is the strategy of Xi Jinping, China.

They have sent a lot of people all over the world, especially the key countries for them to change the opinion of the world. Of course, it's very difficult to change the opinion of the United States of America, but it's a little easier for them to change the opinion of Canada, Australia, New Zealand or weaker EU countries who are suffering from a revenue deficit. I mean, cannot-satisfy-their-people kind of country, for example, Greece or Italy or another one. They (China) are very strategic about that, so it's very difficult. And also, they have worldwide syndicates, so they are a very tough negotiator. I think so.

たち」であり、もう一つが「中国政府を守ろうとする人たち」で、中国からの多くの留学生はこちらに含まれます。ですから、カナダの中国人社会は一つではありません。人数的には香港支持派より、中国本土から来てカナダに住んでいる人のほうが多いのではないかと思います。それが習近平の中国の戦略です。

　彼らは世界の意見を変えるため、世界中に、特に彼らにとって鍵となる国々に、多くの人たちを送り込んでいます。もちろん、アメリカの意見を変えるのは非常に難しいのですが、カナダやオーストラリア、ニュージーランドなどの意見を変えるほうが、もう少し簡単です。あるいは、歳入不足で苦しんでいるＥＵの弱小国ですね。ギリシャやイタリアやその他、国民を満足させることができていないような国です。彼ら（中国）はそうした面で非常に戦略的なので、実に難しいのです。彼らには世界的組織もあり、交渉も非常に上手だと思います。

2 Advice to Supporters of Hong Kong Democratic Protests

Of course, these people who are struggling against Beijing to help Hong Kong people have organizations worldwide, but they are very weak, I think, in the meaning of resources and in the meaning of their opinion and their resort, how to make influence on Chinese government. So, almost all of them are asking for help from other countries, especially from strong countries like G7. But their voices are not welcomed in every country.

But little by little, the supporters are getting more and more people assisting the problem of Hong Kong. For example, I already said in my lecture in Toronto, one Canadian military ship had passed near Hong Kong. It's one demonstration for Beijing China. And before this lecture, they caught the CFO of Huawei at the airport of Canada, and it's very helpful even for me to go to Canada. It means Canada is standing by the U.S. government. It means so. So, it's helpful for us to hold a lecture in Toronto.

もちろん、香港市民を助けるために中国政府と戦っている人たちにも世界的組織はありますが、資金面でも言論面でも、中国政府にいかに影響を与えるかという手段の面でも、きわめて弱いと思います。ですから彼らの大部分は他国に、特にG7のような強い国に助けを求めていますが、その声はどこの国でも歓迎されてはいません。

とはいえ、少しずつ、支持者たちは、香港問題を支援する人々を獲得してきています。たとえば、すでにトロントの説法で述べたように、カナダの軍艦が一隻、香港の近くを通過しました。これは中国政府に対する一つのデモンストレーションです。また説法に先立ち、カナダの空港でファーウェイのCFOが拘束されましたが、これは私にとってもカナダに行くうえで大きな助けになりました。それは「カナダはアメリカ政府の側につく」ことを意味するので、私たちがトロントで講演会を開催するうえで助かりました。

Be patient, and continue to protest using peaceful means

So, firstly I just want to say one thing. Of course, it's related to the second person, maybe. Xi Jinping's China is now thinking about separating what the Hong Kong government did and what Beijing China did, and their main strategy is to show the people of the world, all sorts of TV or newspapers writers, that this is just the confusion in Hong Kong and not the Beijing problem. This is the first strategy. I think so.

So, when I came back to Japan and read some opinion magazines of Japan, some conservative-trend magazine said that this—I mean, "this" means the Hong Kong demonstration-like thing—is like the old-fashioned Japanese students' rebellion against our government. It's my younger age. It's more than 50 years ago, around that. Someone says like that. The conservative people in Japan look at the matter of

2　香港の民主化デモ勢力へのアドバイス

忍耐し、平和的デモの継続を

　そこで、まず言っておきたいことが一つあります。これは二人目の方にも関係あることかもしれませんが、習近平の中国は今、「香港政府がしたこと」と「中国政府がしたこと」を分けようと考えています。彼らの主な戦略は、世界中の様々なテレビや新聞記者たちに対し、「これは香港内部の混乱に過ぎず、中国政府の問題ではない」という見せ方をすることです。これが彼らの第一戦略だと思います。

　日本に帰って来て日本のオピニオン誌をいくつか読んでみると、ある保守系の雑誌では、「この香港デモは、日本で昔流行った学生運動（反政府運動）のようなものだ」と書いていました。それは私が若い頃で、50年以上前か、そのへんのことです。そう言っている人がいました。日本の保守系の人たちは香港の問題を、日本や世界中の大学で昔流行った学生ストライキのような左翼的活動として見ており、そう考えているのです。別の保守

Hong Kong as a left-hand side activity, like the old-fashioned students' strike in universities in Japan and all around the world. They're thinking it's like that one. Another conservative opinion maker said that, "That is Asama Sansou Jiken (incident)," it means the Japanese Red Army's kidnapping and their fight against Japanese police and finally, they were perished by police. So, even the conservative side of Japanese opinionists is saying like that nowadays.

So, it will become the turning point, I think. I guess one is the petrol bomb, it's *kaen-bin* in Japanese. They say that a disguised policeman of Hong Kong did so, but when it broadcasted, people of the world, especially Japanese people, looked at that—one party is policemen shooting and attacking students or civilian people, but on another side, someone threw away the petrol bomb, so it's a not-so-good impression. So, if it's made by Beijing's hidden project, I think so, but it's not so good for the impression

系言論人は、「あれは浅間山荘事件だ」と言っていました。日本の連合赤軍が人質をとって警察と戦い、最終的に警察によって壊滅させられた事件です。日本の保守系言論人さえ、現在、そういう言い方をしています。

ですから、ターニングポイントになると思います。一つには火炎瓶でしょう。「変装した香港警察がやった」と言われていますが、その映像が放送されて、世界の人たちや特に日本人が、「一方では警察官が学生や市民に発砲したり攻撃したりしていて、もう一方では誰かが火炎瓶を投げている」のを見ると、印象はあまり良くありません。それが中国政府の秘密作戦によるものだとしても――たぶんそうだと思いますが――デモから受ける印象としては、あまり良くありません。

2 Advice to Supporters of Hong Kong Democratic Protests

from that demonstration.

So, if they seek for freedom and democracy and peace, please be patient and keep a peaceful demonstration only. They can do, of course, walking or speaking or scattering their writings, it's OK, I think. But don't resist against the violence by violence. It's not so good. It will not get the compassion from other countries, especially the Japanese people who don't like struggle or trouble or conflict. So, be careful.

It's been more than 100 days. It's enough time. When there was the Tiananmen incident, Beijing didn't even have patience to keep silence and peace for 100 days. After that, there came a very important person from a foreign country. After that time, they did Tiananmen incident. So, it's a very difficult time, I think. To get the assistance from another country, don't show the conflict as the inner conflict of Hong Kong only.

2 香港の民主化デモ勢力へのアドバイス

　ですから「自由と民主主義と平和」を求めているのであれば、忍耐し、平和的なデモだけにしてください。歩いたり叫んだりチラシを撒いたりするのは当然、構わないと思いますが、暴力に対し暴力で抵抗しては駄目で、得策ではありません。それでは諸外国の同情は得られませんし、特に日本人は争いやトラブルや対立が好きではありませんので、注意してください。

　もう100日以上続いていますので、十分な時間です。天安門事件のときは、中国政府は100日間も沈黙と平和を守らず、その後、海外から要人が来て、そのあとで天安門事件を起こしています。ですから、非常に難しい時期だと思います。他国の支援を得るためには、この対立を「香港内部だけの対立」のように見せてはいけません。

135

Look at the situation from the objective view of an outside country

And I want to ask the demonstration people of Hong Kong, "Don't hate Hong Kong police or Hong Kong administration." They are also Hong Kong citizens. They are just obeying the order of Beijing, China, Xi Jinping regime. So, never hate the people of Hong Kong who are administrating, but please think, "This is just a problem of what they believe in or obey." This is a problem of system, and this is a problem of Marxism.

Even Xi Jinping is now spoken ill of regarding that he is wanting to replace the position of Mao Tse-tung, the founder of Chinese Communist Party. He is accused of that because (at the military parade in the 70th anniversary celebration) he rode on the same car which Mao Tse-tung used and no other person was in it (the following car). So, he was

他国の視点で情勢の客観視を

　そして、香港でデモをしている人たちに申し上げたい
のは、「香港警察や香港政府を憎んではいけない」とい
うことです。彼らもまた香港市民であり、中国政府、習
近平体制の命令に従っているだけですので、決して香港
の行政側の人たちを憎むのではなく、「何を信じ、何に
従うかの問題に過ぎないのだ」と考えてください。これ
は制度の問題であり、マルクス主義の問題なのです。

　習近平さえ現在、「中国共産党の創始者である毛沢東
に取って代わりたがっている」ということに関して悪口
を言われています。そう糾弾されています。（建国 70 周
年の閲兵式で）毛沢東が使用したのと同じ車に乗り、そ
の（後ろを走る）車には誰も乗っていなかったので、「習
近平は毛沢東の亡霊と一緒に同じ車に乗っていた」と非
難されています。ですから、非常に難しい問題です。

criticized that, "Xi Jinping is riding the same car with the ghost of Mao Tse-tung." He was said like that. So, the problem is very difficult.

Please look at the phenomenon from the viewpoint of other countries' people, I mean, objectively. It's very important. One illustration of that is, don't use petrol bomb. It's not good for the impression to other people of the world. Especially on TV occasion, it's not so good.

The world is following my design

How to destroy the Chinese government is a huge problem, indeed. This October 1, they made a great military march at the Tiananmen Square, and they showed the new ballistic missiles which can attack even the United States of America, and of course the aircraft carriers of the U.S. Such kind of new-type missiles, they showed. If we use forceful thinking, it

2　香港の民主化デモ勢力へのアドバイス

　どうか、他の国の人たちの視点から、すなわち客観的な目で、その現象を見てください。それが非常に重要です。その一例としては、世界の他の人たちにとって印象が良くないので火炎瓶は使わないことです。特にテレビの場合は良くありません。

世界は私のデザイン通りに動いている

　いかにして中国政府を倒すかは、実際、たいへんな問題です。今年10月1日、中国は天安門広場で盛大な軍事パレードを行ない、アメリカの空母は言うまでもなくアメリカ本土も攻撃できる新しい弾道ミサイルを披露しました。そういった新型ミサイルを披露しています。私たちが強硬的な考え方をとった場合は新たな戦争になってしまうので、十分、賢明に考えなければいけません。

will make the next war. So, think very cleverly.

My opinion is, I've been fighting against Xi Jinping during these almost 10 years. When he was the vice president of China, I saw that he's a very dangerous person. After he got his presidency, it came true, and I have been making a surrounding strategy for China. So, we made a good relationship with Donald Trump, the United States, and supported the victory of Republicans.

Also, we want to keep the good connections with Putin Russia, and of course, India, Nepal, Sri Lanka, the Philippines, Malaysia, Australia, and Europe. I have been surrounding Xi Jinping through my foreign activities, speeches, and lectures. I did a lot. And something's happened through my activities, for example, the policy of Australia or America. Canada is, just now. And I went to Germany. I'm making opinions of the world.

And through my mission, I have been giving

2　香港の民主化デモ勢力へのアドバイス

　私の意見としては、習近平とはここ 10 年近く戦って
きました。彼が中国の副主席だった時点で、非常に危険
な人物であることは見抜いていましたが、主席になった
後でそれが現実化したので、中国包囲網を形成してまい
りました。ですからアメリカのドナルド・トランプと良
好な関係を築き、共和党が勝つよう支援しました。

　また、プーチンのロシアや、もちろんインド、ネパー
ル、スリランカ、フィリピン、マレーシア、オーストラ
リア、ヨーロッパとも良い関係を保ちたいと思っていま
す。海外巡錫を通した講演活動で習近平を包囲してきま
した。いろいろなことをやってきて、私の活動によって
起きてきたことがあります。たとえばオーストラリアや
アメリカの政策がそうですし、カナダは今まさにその最
中です。ドイツにも行きました。世界のオピニオンは私
がつくっているのです。

　また、自分の使命を通して、日本のマスメディアにも

141

opinion to our mass media. And Japan is also in the middle way now because we have a military alliance with the United States, but at the second time, we have an economic problem, so nothing strong deeds can be done by our government. They are just inviting the customers from Asian area, especially mainland China.

Japanese people cannot divide mainland China, Hong Kong, and Taiwan. But I think clearly, and in Taiwan this March, I said clearly what's the difference between mainland China and Taiwan, and in case of Hong Kong crisis, please help Hong Kong people. I asked Taiwanese people at that time. All are in my design and direction now.

A complicated strategy to surround China through opinion and economy

But this fighting is a very huge one, so we need a

意見を伝えてきました。日本も今、途中段階にあります。日本はアメリカと軍事同盟を結んではいますが、二番目の要素として経済問題があるため、日本政府は何も強い行動を取ることができずにいます。ただ、中国本土を中心とするアジア地域から買い物客を呼び込んでいるだけです。

　日本人は中国本土も香港も台湾も区別がつかないのですが、私は明確に考えていますし、今年の３月には台湾で、中国と台湾の違いとは何かについて明言しました。そして「香港危機が起きた場合は香港の人たちを助けてください」と、台湾の人たちにそのときお願いしました。現在、すべては私がデザインして示したとおりに動いています。

言論面や経済面も含む複雑な「中国包囲戦略」

　しかし、これは非常に大きな戦いですので、包囲戦略

surrounding strategy and we need, in the meaning of opinion, to surround Beijing China and criticize what is wrong. Its beginning is the one-party system of communism. It's the origin. And Xi Jinping is just aiming at being like Mao Tse-tung or China's First Emperor-like person. I published a lot of books regarding this matter, through Xi Jinping's guardian spirit's words.* So, Japanese people, including politics and the mass media, know a lot from my books, but they can do nothing.

In addition to that, there was a tax hike on this October 1—it's the consumption tax, from eight percent to ten percent. Today is just 11 days after the tax hike, but today's newspaper reported that even the 7-Eleven chain stores are scheduled to close or relocate 1,000 stores. It's a huge one. And Sogo and Seibu departments, some of them are scheduled to close. It means, there comes the consumption depression.

---

* The author has already published a total of five books of spiritual interviews with the guardian spirit of Xi Jinping, including *Jiyu no Tame ni, Tatakau beki wa Ima* (lit. "Now is the Time to Fight for Freedom") (Tokyo: IRH Press, 2019) and *Xi Jinping Shugorei Uyghur Dan'atsu wo Kataru* (lit. "The Guardian Spirit of Xi Jinping Speaks on Suppression of Uyghurs") (Tokyo: IRH Press, 2018).

が必要ですし、言論面でも中国政府を包囲して、どこが間違っているのかを批判する必要があります。中国の始まりは共産主義による一党独裁です。そこが原点で、習近平が目指しているのはまさに、毛沢東や始皇帝のような人物になることです。この点に関しては、習近平守護霊の言葉を通して本を何冊も出したので（注）、日本人は、政治家やマスメディアも含めて、私の本を通して多くを知ってはいるのですが、何もすることができずにいます。

　それに加えて、この10月1日には増税があり、消費税が8パーセントから10パーセントになりました。今日は増税されてからまだ11日目ですが、今日の新聞には「セブン–イレブンさえ1000店舗を閉店または移転する予定である」とありました。大変な規模です。そごう・西武もいくつか閉店を予定しており、これは消費不況が来ることを意味しています。

(注)習近平守護霊の霊言を収録した本として、『自由のために、戦うべきは今』『習近平守護霊　ウイグル弾圧を語る』（共に幸福の科学出版刊）等、計5冊を発刊している。

Recently, we are weighted, so Mr. Prime Minister Abe must be just thinking about next year's Olympics, and at that time, he expects the economic growth of Japan again. So, Japanese government people and the opposite parties also don't work about this Hong Kong matter. Only we did and said a lot. It means we don't get votes from common people because to criticize gigantic China means inviting greater depressions for us.

So, we must overcome this problem. One should be to recognize that the hike of consumption tax was a failure. We repeatedly insisted that it's not time for us to raise consumption tax. Our economic growth is only one percent, or recently, only zero percent. If we made a raise of consumption tax, it would make our economy destroyed.

We have 2 times of governmental deficit compared to our total GDP, but Beijing China also has officially 2.5 times governmental deficit, or someone said 4

最近、税金が重くなったので、安倍首相は来年オリンピックが来れば日本経済が再び成長すると期待しており、そのことしか頭にないはずですので、日本政府も野党も香港問題に取り組んではいません。いろいろ行動や発言を重ねているのは私たちだけで、それは一般国民から票が入らないことを意味しています。巨大な中国を批判すれば、さらなる不況を招くからです。

私たちはこの問題を乗り越えなければなりません。一つには、「消費増税は失敗であった」と認めるべきです。私たちが繰り返し主張してきたのは、「今は消費税を上げるときではない。日本の経済成長率はわずか１パーセントであり、最近はゼロパーセントである。消費税を上げれば日本経済は崩壊する」ということです。

日本政府の財政赤字はGDP（国内総生産）の２倍ですが、中国の財政赤字は公式にはGDPの2.5倍で、人によっては４倍だと言っています。ですから、これは、「日

times government deficit, as much as their GDP. So, this is a chicken game: Japan or China, which is faster to be destroyed in the economic meaning? This is a very difficult game. I'm thinking about that.

China had made One Belt, One Road strategy. But it's at the verge of ruining now. I know about that. Mr. Kuroda, President of the Bank of Japan, made a great loan to developing countries, and he's making a competition with China's that kind of economic strategy. We are fighting in the level of economics and in the level of international monetary field. I'm suggesting a lot about that. We have our political party, and Mr. Abe's plans are almost the same as what we dispatched. Only the tax hike was too early because of declining of the economy. So, we have also the same political problem. But maybe this is not their concern about their fighting.

We have a very complicated strategy, and are fighting in a lot of aspects; just, it's a surrounding

本と中国のどちらが先に経済崩壊を迎えるか」という〝チキン・レース〟なのです。実に厳しいゲームで、私はそのことを考えています。

　中国には「一帯一路戦略」がありましたが、もはや崩れかかっていることが私には見えています。日銀の黒田総裁は発展途上国に多額の貸し出しをして、中国のそうした経済戦略と競争しています。経済のレベル、国際金融のレベルで戦っているわけです。それについては私からいろいろ提言もしています。私たちには自前の政党があり、安倍さんのプランは私たちが発信したのとほぼ同じものですが、増税だけは、経済が傾いているので時期尚早でした。ですから日本も同じような政治問題を抱えているわけですが、香港の人たちが自分たちの戦いについて抱いている関心とは違うかもしれません。

　私たちには非常に複雑な戦略があり、さまざまな側面の戦いをしています。まさに「中国包囲戦略」です。こ

strategy for China. It's a great strategy, so I said—I didn't say the name of the country, but I already said at the lecture of Toronto that I will finish the totalitarian regime of China from 2020 to 2030. It's our fighting for them. All of the Happy Science Group is concentrating on this problem. So, in the near future, we will overcome their ambition. I think so. Please rely on me about that.

Then, I just ask you for the repetition of the Hong Kong demonstration. Please be careful about that. Now, for example, just as I planned, the Uyghur people are scheduled to be protected by the U.S. government. I let them know a lot about that kind of great suffering. So, the future will be brighter. But it's another problem. I just want to say we'll do our best, and I will tell in every chance that I want to assist the Hong Kong people's freedom. But be careful acting. Never show your weak points to Beijing or other media. I hope so.

れは大きな戦略であり、私はトロントの説法で、国の名前は言いませんでしたが、「中国の全体主義体制を2020年から2030年までの間に終わらせる」と述べました。それが私たちの戦いです。幸福の科学は全グループを挙げてこの問題に集中していますので、近い将来、彼らの野望を打ち負かすことができると思います。それに関しては信頼していただければと思います。

　ですから、香港のデモを繰り返すようお願いしますが、慎重になってください。現在、たとえば私の計画どおり、ウイグルの人たちはアメリカ政府に守ってもらえる方向になっています。そうしたひどい苦しみについていろいろ知らせましたので、未来は明るいでしょう。それはまた別の問題ですが、「私たちは全力を尽くす」ということだけは申し上げておきたいと思います。あらゆる機会に、香港の自由を支援したいと伝えていこうと思いますが、注意深く行動してください。決して中国政府や他のメディアに弱みを見せないことを願っています。

3 Answer to Ms. Sheng: The Plan to Realize a Free China within the Next 10 Years

Fujii Thank you for your precious advice for us and Ms. Gloria Fung. We will move on to the next question.

The second person was Ms. Sheng Xue, one of the prominent Chinese human rights activists and vice chairperson of the Federation for a Democratic China. For two years, we had a good relationship with her and her organization. At first, she visited our political party, Happiness Realization Party, during her visit to Japan two years ago, and we have been keeping in touch. Then, this time, it was her first time to attend Master's event, so she was very pleased to join it. As you told us in your lecture (entitled "What I thought in Canada") yesterday, she invited Ms. Kobayashi the night before the event.

3 盛雪氏への回答
──次の10年で「自由な中国」を
実現するための計画は

藤井　私たちとグロリア・ファンさんに貴重なアドバイスをありがとうございます。次の質問に移らせていただきます。

　二人目の方は盛雪さんです。著名な中国人人権活動家の一人で、「民主中国陣線」の副主席です。私たちは2年前から彼女と彼女の団体と良好な関係にあります。最初は2年前に来日されたとき、私たち幸福実現党を訪ねてこられました。以来、連絡を取り合い、総裁先生の講演会に参加されるのは今回が初めてで、非常に喜んで参加されました。昨日、総裁先生が御法話（『カナダで考えたこと』）で言われたように、彼女は講演会の前日の夜に、小林さんを招待してくれました。

Ryuho Okawa Oh, yeah, brave. She's brave.

Fujii [*Laughs.*] Yes, she had a dinner with them. She will explain about that.

Kobayashi A lot of Chinese activists gathered at her place, and they had a discussion on the unity of groups to fight against the Chinese Communist Party's tyranny. Her house was like a shelter for people who have fled to Canada. So, once they arrive in Toronto, they will go to her house, so that they have a place to stay. I think she is a very loving person to protect all the people who have escaped from China.

I asked them, "Which party in Canada do you support? Conservative Party of Canada or The Liberal Party?" and their answer was, "Conservative Party." I asked the reason why, and they said that, "Because Prime Minister Trudeau doesn't have any idea for Chinese issues." And his father, Pierre Trudeau,

大川隆法　ああ、勇気がありますね。勇敢な方です。

藤井　（笑）はい。そして夕食をご一緒しましたので、彼女からご説明します。

小林　彼女の自宅に中国人活動家が大勢集まって、中国共産党政府の圧政に対抗するために、いかにして民主活動グループを団結させるかについて話し合っていました。彼女の自宅はカナダに逃げてきた人の避難所のようになっているそうです。彼らはトロントに着くと、泊まる場所を求めて彼女の家に来るのです。中国から逃げてきた人なら誰でも守ろうとする、愛に溢れた方だと思います。

　「カナダのどの政党を支持しますか。保守党ですか、カナダ自由党ですか」と彼らに尋ねたところ、保守党との答えでした。理由を聞くと、「今のトルドー首相には中国問題について何も考えがないから」と言っていました。彼の父親のピエール・トルドーは、かなり親中国だったので、彼らによれば「トルドー首相は父親がしたこと

was so pro-China. So, they said, "He just wants to do something that his father did." That's why they couldn't support him.

And they're hoping that, if the Conservative Party wins in the coming election, the relationship between Canada and the United States would become much closer. That means Canada will follow President Trump's Chinese policies. That's the reason why they supported the Conservative Party. We had a great discussion. Also, they hoped your lecture to be very successful, so we made a wish together for the success of your event on the following day. So, may I ask you her questions?

Ryuho Okawa Uh huh.

Kobayashi She had two questions. First, she wanted to know about Master's plan for Chinese people to enjoy happiness and freedom without persecution

を自分もしたいだけ」だから支持はできないとのことでした。

　彼らの希望としては、来る選挙で保守党が勝てばカナダとアメリカの関係がずっと近くなるだろうということです。つまり、カナダがトランプ大統領の中国政策を後追いすることになるので、彼らは保守党を支持しているのです。私たちはいろいろ話し合うことができましたし、皆さん、総裁先生の講演会の大成功を願ってくださり、翌日の講演会の成功を共に祈りました。そこで、彼女の質問をしてもよろしいでしょうか。

大川隆法　はい。

小林　彼女には二つ質問がありました。一つは、総裁先生のご計画が知りたいということです。中国国民が中国共産党から迫害されずに幸福と自由を享受するための計

from Chinese Communist Party. A lot of people are suffering, as she said, so she would like you to tell us your plan to set them free.

And the second question was, you talked a little about it (in the lecture in Toronto), but she thinks that Japan is a great nation. She used the words, "a democratic torch in Asia." She had great expectations for Japan. But she feels like what Japan does is not enough. So, she was willing to ask you how Japan can do better and give more effort to fulfill its mission.

Canada should adopt the Benjamin Franklin spirit

Ryuho Okawa OK. It's also a very difficult problem. Maybe it's beyond their power today. I hope also for the victory of Conservative Party of Canada. It's Mr. Scheer's victory. If we can get such victory, there is a conservative line: Boris Johnson and Mr. Scheer and Donald Trump. These three guys are very powerful

画です。「多くの人が苦しんでいるので、彼らを自由にするためのご計画を教えてほしい」とのことでした。

二問目は、（トロント講演会でも）少しお話しされましたが、彼女も日本は素晴らしい国だと思っています。「アジアの民主主義の松明」という言葉を使って、日本に大きな期待を寄せているのですが、「日本がやっていることは十分ではない」と感じており、「どうしたら日本は、その使命を果たすために、より良いことができ、より多くの努力ができるのか」をお聞きしたいそうです。

カナダに「ベンジャミン・フランクリン精神」を

大川隆法　わかりました。こちらも非常に難しい問題です。今の彼女たちの力を超えているかもしれません。私もカナダ保守党の勝利を願っています。シーア氏の勝利です。そちらが勝利すれば保守のラインができます。ボリス・ジョンソンとシーア氏とドナルド・トランプで、この三人は対・共産党として非常に強いと思います。

159

on the communist party. I think so.

I had a plan to realize that. But our followers in Toronto, or Canada, are not so great, so in the election meaning, we don't have enough power for that. So, I just want to say the mistakes of Prime Minister Trudeau. We can criticize about that, and it's good for Mr. Scheer to become the next prime minister. He is powerful now. Mr. Trudeau changed his political attitude these days, but Mr. Trudeau is still strong in Canada, so we need another "God's wind" like when we experienced Donald Trump's victory.

Canada's weak point, I already told about that. Mr. Trudeau likes to be liberal, it's from his father. But to be liberal does not mean to be democratic. Democracy is not always liberal. In these times, in the United States also, Canada also, and other European countries, "liberal" means sometimes a labor party- or communist-like thinking.

3 次の10年で「自由な中国」を実現するための計画は

　それを実現する計画があったのですが、トロントという
かカナダの当会信者は、あまり多くありません。選挙
という観点では、それだけの力が十分にありませんので、
トルドー首相の間違いを指摘するにとどめたいと思いま
す。それを批判することならできますし、シーア氏が次
の首相になるうえでも役立つでしょう。彼は今、力を持っ
ています。トルドー氏は最近、政治姿勢を変えています
が、カナダではまだ有力ですので、私たちとしては、ド
ナルド・トランプの勝利を経験したときのような「神風」
が再び必要です。

　カナダの弱点については、すでにお話ししました。ト
ルドー氏は父親ゆずりのリベラル好みですが、「リベラ
ル」がすなわち民主主義的ということではありません。
民主主義はリベラルであるとは限らなくて、今の時代の
リベラルとは、アメリカでもカナダでも、その他のヨー
ロッパ諸国でも、労働党や共産党のような考え方を意味
することがあるのです。

161

3 The Plan to Realize a Free China within the Next 10 Years

So, we must stop "liberal" to some extent, and change it to the direction of how to make their country stronger in the meaning of liberal. It's a Benjamin Franklin spirit, I think. In the meaning of Benjamin Franklin's spirit, to be liberal is good, but if we use "liberal" to save people by dint of government's power only—give money, scattering money only, or buy votes by scattering money—this "liberal" leads to hell. I want to say so.

Mr. Trudeau's father is not a god. I also want to add it. Canada is a good country, but its diversity and its tolerance are enough, and over-enough, indeed. If it's combined with too much liberal, it means Canada will be led to communist party-like country, or Sweden-like country in the meaning of environmentalists. It's almost the same.

ですから、ある程度のところで「リベラル」を押しとどめ、「自由主義的」（リベラル）という意味において、どうやって自分たちの国を強くしていくかという方向に変えていかないといけません。それは「ベンジャミン・フランクリン精神」だと思います。ベンジャミン・フランクリン精神という意味での「自由主義的」なら良いけれども、「リベラル」という言葉を、政府の力で人を救うだけとか、お金を与えてバラまくだけとか、バラまいて票を買うなどの意味で使うとしたら、「そういうリベラルは地獄に通じる」と言っておきたいと思います。

トルドー氏の父は神ではないということも付け加えておきたいと思います。カナダは良い国ではありますが、多様性と寛容性はもう十分であり、実際には十分すぎます。それが行きすぎたリベラルと結びついた場合は、カナダは共産党国家のような国か、環境保護主義者という意味でスウェーデンのような国になるでしょう。それとほぼ同じものなのです。

3 The Plan to Realize a Free China within the Next 10 Years

A long timespan of planning to change the Earth

It was told that there is a 16-year-old lady who insists on environments and global warming. She was supported by two groups, one of which is assisted by Chinese money, I've heard. So, it's the strategy of Xi Jinping China. He uses environment and global warming. In China, there are very much emissions of CO_2 through their coal-powered electricity, but it's a hidden part. They just want to weaken Donald Trump's America First policy. That's their aim. So, Chinese government uses only, a 16-year-old, just a small girl. It's their way.

I said that (problem of) environment is quite different. I said Donald Trump is true. CO_2 emission does not have strong influence on us. If you want to stop all the CO_2 by 2050, please save the poverty of the people instead. They need food, they need industry. It's important. I said so.

地球の変化は長いスパンで計画されている

　自然環境と地球温暖化について主張している16歳の女性がいることが伝えられています。彼女は二つのグループから支持されていて、その一つは中国マネーの援助を受けているということです。これが習近平の中国の戦略で、環境と地球温暖化を利用しているわけです。中国では石炭を燃やす火力発電によるCO_2排出量が非常に多いのですが、その点は隠されています。彼らはドナルド・トランプの「アメリカ・ファースト」政策を弱めたいだけなのです。それが狙いであって、中国政府はまだ16歳の少女を利用しているだけなのです。これが彼らのやり方です。

　私は、「環境問題はかなり違っており、ドナルド・トランプは正しい」とお話ししました。CO_2排出の影響はさほど大きなものではありません。2050年までにCO_2排出を全廃しようと考えるくらいなら、それより、人々を貧困から救ってください。彼らには食べ物や産業が必要であり、それが非常に重要なことなのです。そう

3 The Plan to Realize a Free China within the Next 10 Years

Global warming is not the only reason of this Earth's climate. I know a lot about that. We have designed the long timespan of planning to change this Earth and how to make civilization prosper on this Earth. So, what she said is not right. I said so.

But Canadian people like environment. They like beaver, they like reindeer, like that. So, they are living in heaven with animals, maybe heavenly animals. So, my wife said when we visited Canada, "They need sixth dimensional world and seventh dimensional world in Canada." We could see only fourth dimensional world and fifth dimensional world. Where is the sixth dimensional world, where is the seventh dimensional world, or where is the eighth dimensional world in the air of Canada? We could not find anyone in that area like Australia when we visited it. We could not see anyone in that

述べました。

　地球気候の要因は、地球温暖化だけではありません。私はそれについては、よく知っているのです。私たちは長いスパンで、この地球の変化を計画し、地球上にどうやって文明を繁栄させるかをデザインしてきましたので、彼女が言ったことは正しくありません。そうお話ししました。

　ただ、カナダの人たちは自然環境が好きです。ビーバーやトナカイなども好きなので、たぶん天国では、天国的な動物たちと一緒に住んでいるのだと思います。ですから家内は、カナダに行ったとき、「カナダには六次元世界や七次元世界が必要です」と言っていました。四次元世界や五次元世界しか見えないので、「カナダの上空のどこに、六次元や七次元や八次元の世界があるのか」と。以前に訪れたオーストラリアと同じく、その領域に誰もいませんでした。カナダには、たった二百年ほどの非常に短い歴史しかないからです。

area because they have only 200 years or so, very short history.

So, I said there is no god in some meaning because of course, the ancient worldwide God is watching them, but Mr. Trudeau's father is not a god, of course. Alexander Wood is also not a god. So, I want our Happy Science Canadian members to become a greater person and make the world of angels in the heaven of Canada. I hope so.

And, our fighting way is to change policy of Mr. Trudeau and to assist Mr. Scheer. Even if we fail in this election—it's only 10 more days, so it's not enough, I think, but our activities will change Canada in the near future. And Mr. Trudeau also will change his mind; if it's bad or it's not so effective, he will change his mind. This is the political activities in Canada, we hope so.

ですから私は、「ある意味で、神はいない」と言いました。もちろん、古くからの世界的な神はカナダを見てはいますが、トルドー氏の父親は神ではありませんし、アレキサンダー・ウッドも無論、神ではありませんので、カナダの幸福の科学信者がますます偉大な人物となって、カナダの天国に天使の世界をつくってくださることを願っています。

私たちの戦い方としては、トルドー氏の政策を変えさせてシーア氏を支援することです。今度の選挙でうまくいかなくても——あと10日しかないので十分ではないと思いますが、幸福の科学の活動が近い将来、カナダを変えるでしょう。トルドーさんも、自分の考えがまずかったり効果がない場合は考えを変えるでしょう。そういうかたちでカナダでは政治活動をしていきたいと考えています。

The danger of a surveillance society ruled by AI

Ryuho Okawa And she asked me the plan? How to dissolve China?

Kobayashi Yes, your plan to liberate, to make Chinese people enjoy freedom and happiness.

Ryuho Okawa Ah, it's a great problem, but the end is coming, I think. People, I mean even the people of Communists are hating the one-party system and Xi Jinping's dictatorship. As you know, there are a lot of cameras which are surveying the people, surveillance cameras, and these become 600 million cameras next year, I mean 2020. 1.4 billion people are watched by 0.6 billion cameras means two people are watched by one camera, almost. No one can think about such kind of *1984*-like, George Orwell's telescreen society. It's a society of fear; fearful society came

AIによる監視社会の危険性

大川隆法　それと、彼女の質問は、中国を解体する計画についてでしたか。

小林　はい。中国の人たちを解放し、自由と幸福を享受していただくための計画です。

大川隆法　ああ、それは大きな問題ですが、終わりは近づいていると思います。共産党の人たちも、一党制度と習近平の独裁を嫌っています。ご存じのように、国民を監視するカメラがたくさんあり、来年2020年には6億台にもなるそうです。6億台のカメラで14億人を監視するということは、ほぼ二人につきカメラ1台の割合で監視されるわけで、こんな、ジョージ・オーウェルの『1984年』に出てくるテレスクリーン社会みたいになるとは、考えられないことです。まさに恐怖社会ですね。恐怖社会の再来です。

3 The Plan to Realize a Free China within the Next 10 Years

again.

The real god of China is AI. AI can decide almost everything. It's very fearful. So, we can make such kind of opinion: If people want to be free, we don't need any cameras watching us, or don't need to check every person's money's working through the electronic system. Just the controlling is everything. It's also a fearful future.

So, someone must say about another George Orwell-like warning to them. They think that, "We are a very advanced country because we can use AI and we can make slave our 1.4 billion people through AI system," but it's not good for fundamental human rights. To be free is, you can be free to think about and to walk about and to choose anything.

So, our next project is to make collapse within them by dint of our thinking or thought. "Are you happy or not?" We'll ask them and change them. Chinese people will come to Japan, but at that time,

3　次の10年で「自由な中国」を実現するための計画は

　中国の本当の神はAI（人工知能）です。AIがほとんど何でも決めることができるというのは非常に恐ろしいことなので、私たちとしては、「人は自由になりたければ、自分たちを監視するカメラなど要らないし、電子システムによって一人ひとりのお金の動きをチェックする必要もない」という意見を発信していくことができます。「管理がすべて」というのも、やはり恐ろしい未来です。

　ですから、誰かが、現代のジョージ・オーウェルのように彼らに警告しなければいけません。彼らは、「自分たちはAIを使えるから非常に先進国であり、AIシステムで14億人を奴隷にすることができる」と思っていますが、それは基本的人権にとっては良いことではありません。自由であるとは、「自由に考え、自由に移動し、何でも選択することができる」ということだからです。

　私たちの次なるプロジェクトは、「思想の力」によって彼らを内側から崩壊させることです。「あなたは幸福ですか、どうですか」と問いかけて、彼らを変えていくのです。日本に来た中国人に、「そういう社会に生きて

173

we can ask them and influence them. "Are you really happy in your society? Is this a human society or the society of happiness? If not, you should change it. If not, it's because of the difference of aim of your country. Your head of the country is just aiming at controlling people. Just controlling people means peaceful for government-side person, but common people are not happy and peaceful."

It's like the Nazism-like society. It's like the Lenin- and Stalin-like regime's style. Chinese people are not the Jewish people who were killed by Hitler. Xi Jinping is now a new Hitler who can kill 1.4 billion people. If they don't obey his order, he can kill everyone. And he is also controlling the opinion or the communication of every person through a lot of intelligent police. Hundreds of thousands of people are working for intelligence police. And to criticize the system will ruin their regime, I think. I already told them at the Toronto lecture that one is mass

いて本当に幸福ですか。それは人間的で幸福な社会ですか。そうでないのなら変えるべきです。それは、あなたの国が目指しているものが違うからです。あなたの国のトップは国民をコントロールすることしか目指していません。国民がコントロールされるだけというのは、政府の側にとっては〝平和〟であっても、一般国民は幸福でも平和でもありません」と問いかけて、彼らに影響を与えていくことができます。

それはナチズムに似た社会であり、レーニン体制やスターリン体制的なスタイルです。中国の人たちは、ヒットラーに殺されたユダヤ人ではないのです。今の習近平は、14億人の命を奪うことのできる「新たなヒットラー」です。自分の命令に従わない相手は誰でも殺せるわけです。彼はまた、大人数の情報警察によって、国民全員の意見や通信内容をコントロールしています。情報警察の職員が何十万人もいます。そのシステムを批判することで、彼らの体制を滅ぼすことができると思います。トロントの説法でも言いましたが、第一に「大量殺戮」、第二に「秘密警察」、第三に「強制収容所」、これらがヒッ

murder, second is the secret police, and the third is a concentration camp. These are the characteristic points of a totalitarian regime, a dictatorship regime like Hitler or Stalin, I already said so in Taiwan. So, it's a battle of thinking, a battle of opinion.

Above economy and politics lies God's justice

So, Japanese people, just stop thinking about money or income only. We must think about politics. And above politics, there is God's justice! This is what Happy Science is teaching Japanese people. Japanese people or Japanese government think about economy and income and money only. We were told that Japanese are "economic animals" before we experienced the great depression through 1990's. We are told that Japanese are economic animals. Now, still, its criticism can survive if we cannot change our mind. We must seek for world justice, God's justice,

トラーやスターリンのような全体主義体制、独裁体制の特徴です。台湾の説法でもこれを言いました。これは思想戦であり、言論戦なのです。

経済や政治の上に「神の正義」がある

「日本人は、お金や収入のことばかり考えるのをやめなくてはいけない。政治について考えなければいけない。そして、政治の上には『神の正義』がある」ということを、幸福の科学は日本人に教えています。日本人や日本政府は、経済や収入、お金のことしか考えていません。日本人は、1990年代の大不況を経験する前から「エコノミック・アニマル」と言われていました。「日本人はエコノミック・アニマルである」と言われているのです。その批判は、私たちの心が変わらない限り、今も生きています。私たちは「世界正義」を求め、「神の正義」を求め、責任を持たねばなりません。それが非常に大切なことです。

177

3 The Plan to Realize a Free China within the Next 10 Years

and have responsibility. It's very important.

I saw almost the same thing in Canada. Canada has some kind of freedom and tolerance, indeed, but I felt a little responsibility. Of course, they think, "We are a not-so-large country and have a not-so-large population, so we don't have enough power worldwide." They should think so, but it's the same in Japan also. Canada and Japan also, we belong to G7, and we must have responsibility and want to say something to China who does not belong to G7.

The United Nations permanent members are five countries: The United States of America, the U.K., France, China, and Russia. China and Russia are always the problem. So, we must remake this system also. It was just active at the end of World War II, but now it's not active, it's not effective. We must change this UN. Japan has been the No.1 or No.2 country of "happiness planting" (contribution) for the UN, but we don't have enough opinion to speak to them.

カナダでも同じようなことを目にしました。カナダには確かに、ある種の「自由」や「寛容さ」はありますが、「責任」は少ししか感じられませんでした。もちろん彼らは、「自分たちはそう大きな国ではないし、人口が多くもないので、世界レベルの十分な力はない」と考えているのでしょうが、日本も同じです。カナダも日本もG7に入っていますので、責任を持って、G7に入っていない中国に対して意見を言っていきたいと思います。

国連の常任理事国はアメリカ、イギリス、フランス、中国、ロシアの五カ国ですが、中国とロシアが常に問題になるので、この制度も作り直さなければ駄目です。第二次世界大戦の終戦当時は機能していましたが、現在では機能しておらず実効性もないので、国連を改革しなくてはいけません。日本は国連への〝植福〟（分担金）で一位か二位の国ですが、十分な意見を持てていませんので、国連に対しても物を言っていかないといけません。日本の意見を受け入れないのであれば、財政面で国連を

3 The Plan to Realize a Free China within the Next 10 Years

So, we must say something to the UN. If they won't receive our opinions, we don't support them in the meaning of budget. We must be a politician in this meaning and must be stronger than we used to be. So, these things I'm thinking about.

In this meaning, we, Happy Science, need a lot of members, more members, and more branches all over the world, and of course, have more power in Japan also. But our age will come in the near future. We will change the world, next 10 years. It's my answer.

支えるのはやめることです。この点は政治的に立ち回り、これまでよりもっと強く出なければ駄目です。そうしたことを考えています。

　その意味で、幸福の科学には多くの信者、もっと多くの信者が必要ですし、世界中にもっと多くの支部が必要です。もちろん日本国内でも、もっと力を持つ必要がありますが、近い将来に私たちの時代が来るでしょう。次の10年間で世界を変えます。以上がお答えです。

4 Answer to Ms. Turdush: A Message to Fighters Who Have Faith in God

Fujii Then we are moving on to the third person. She is Rukiye Turdush, former president of Canadian Uyghur Society. She is an enthusiastic activist. A few years ago, she found Master's book online. She already read *Into the Storm of International Politics* and told us that Master is great and she is big fan of Master. Her impression of the book was, "Master's view on world affair is very clear and to the point." She is very close to our team. Ms. Kobayashi will explain our relation with her.

Kobayashi Yes. On the next day, she invited me to her house. It's two hours' drive. That means she drove two hours to attend your lecture. And she said, after she read the book *Into the Storm of International Politics*, she was very impressed. Even though she

4　トールダッシュ氏への回答
　　──戦う信仰者たちへのメッセージ

藤井　それでは、三番目の方に移らせていただきます。ルキエ・トールダッシュさんという「カナダ・ウイグル協会」の前会長で、熱心な活動家です。彼女は数年前にインターネットで総裁先生の本に出会い、すでに『国際政治を見る眼』を読まれています。「総裁先生はすごい。大ファンです」とおっしゃっていました。ご著書の印象として、「国際問題に対する視点が非常に明快で、的を射ている」とのことです。私たちのチームとは非常に親しい関係です。小林さんから説明させていただきます。

小林　はい。私は翌日、車で２時間ほどのところにある彼女の家に招待されました。ですから、彼女は車で２時間かけてやってきて講演会に参加されたわけです。「『国際政治を見る眼』を読んでたいへん感銘を受けた」とおっしゃっていました。ニューヨークでの講演会には行けな

missed your lecture in New York, she was thinking to herself that if you, Master, ever come back to New York, she was willing to attend from Canada to New York, just for your lecture. So, when I invited her to the event, she was super happy and decided to attend on the spot. She was looking forward to your visit for a long time.

Fujii This February, she was invited to an event at McMaster University as a speaker. But some student protesters from China interrupted her. It was a kind of incident, so even the U.S. media covered it. So, she is very famous for her anti–communism activity as an Uyghur.

Kobayashi It showed that there are so many Chinese student groups in Canada, which are against those activists. So, all those three people are really fighting against Chinese Communist Party in spite of repeated

かったので、もし、また総裁先生がニューヨークに来られるなら、彼女はカナダからニューヨークに行って講演会に参加したいと思っていたそうです。ですから、私が講演会にお誘いすると、ものすごく喜ばれて、その場で参加を決めました。トロント御巡錫は彼女が長い間、心待ちにしていたことだったと思います。

藤井　２月にはマクマスター大学での講演に招かれましたが、抗議する中国人学生に妨害されて、ちょっとした騒動になり、アメリカのメディアもこの出来事を取り上げました。それほど、共産主義に反対するウイグル人の活動家として有名な方です。

小林　そのことからもわかるように、カナダには、こうした活動家に反対する中国人学生グループがたくさんあります。この方たちは三人とも、そういうグループの度重なる妨害にもかかわらず、本当に中国共産党と戦って

185

interference from those groups.

Her question was that, a lot of Uyghur people as well as Tibetans, Inner-Mongolians, and Christians in underground churches are suffering under severe oppression. They are losing hope because of the oppression. But she believes that no devil can defeat God. She believes that she's always on the winning side as long as she's with God, so she has very strong faith in God. Could you please give your message to those fighters who have faith in God? Thank you.

The world is now changing after I gave lectures in Germany and Taiwan

Ryuho Okawa OK, OK, OK. Ms. Rukiye Turdish who came from Uyghur. Yes, I'm very much impressed from her interview. She is a religious person, so I also was moved by her voice. She said, "Allah and Elohim are the same. And we sometimes

いる方たちです。

　彼女の質問ですが、多くのウイグル人やチベットや内モンゴルの人たち、地下キリスト教会の信者が、厳しい圧政のもとで苦しんでおり、希望を失いかけているそうです。しかし、彼女は「神に勝てる悪魔はいない」と信じています。「神と共にある限り、自分は常に勝利の側にいる」と信じています。神への非常に強い信仰心をお持ちなのです。神への信仰を持って戦う人たちへのメッセージをいただけますでしょうか。ありがとうございます。

ドイツと台湾での説法が世界を変えつつある

大川隆法　オーケー、オーケー、わかりました。ウイグル出身のルキエ・トールダッシュさんですね。はい。彼女のインタビューには非常に感銘を受けました。宗教的な方なので、私も彼女の声に心を動かされました。「アッラーとエローヒムは同じであり、エローヒムに祈ること

187

pray for Elohim," she said. It's a good point.

I firstly heard about the problem of Uyghur last summer, not this year, but the previous year's end of the summer or September. Activists of Uyghur problem came to our Happiness Realization Party and said that, "We asked Prime Minister Abe or around him about the problem of Uyghur, but Mr. Abe or the LDP, Liberal Democratic Party, did nothing. So, we need help of Master Ryuho Okawa." I've heard that, so I made a lecture last October in Germany and I firstly referred to East Turkistan problem—formally, it's East Turkistan problem, but almost all Japanese don't know about that, so "Uyghur problem".

There are millions of people who are suffering from the persecution from Beijing, China, like the Jewish people were done from Adolf Hitler. I said so. After last October's lecture, two or three days later, China's government admitted that there was a

もあります」と言っていましたが、これは大切なポイントです。

　私が最初にウイグル問題のことを聞いたのは去年の夏でした。今年ではなく、去年の夏の終わりか9月でした。ウイグル問題の活動家が幸福実現党に来られて、「安倍首相やその周辺にウイグル問題のことを頼んだが、安倍さんも自民党も何もしてくれないので、大川隆法総裁に助けていただきたいのです」と言ってこられたと聞いたので、昨年10月にドイツで説法したとき、初めて東トルキスタン問題に言及しました。正式には「東トルキスタン問題」ですが、ほとんどの日本人は（その国名を）知らないでしょうから「ウイグル問題」です。

　アドルフ・ヒットラーに迫害されたユダヤ人のように、中国政府の迫害に苦しんでいる人が何百万人もいると（説法で）話したのですが、昨年10月のその説法の2、3日後に中国政府は、ウイグル人の強制収容所があることを認めました。公式にそう認めたのです。ただ、同時

concentration camp of Uyghur people. They formally admitted that. But at that time, they said, "We are just educating. Educating because, Uyghur people, if they are educated through their own culture only, they cannot get jobs from other Chinese companies, and they cannot enter the universities of China. So, we want to change their education and teach them Chinese, and in addition, to train how to behave like Chinese." They said so. But they admitted to the concentration camp.

I referred to this problem again, this March, in my Taiwan lecture, and at that time, also, I referred to Hong Kong problem. "Taiwan should be Taiwan. 'One country, two systems' doesn't work. So, please keep your freedom, democracy, and prosperity," I said to them. At that time, Tsai Ing-wen had a lesser power, but now, she recovered again, and she will win in the next election. I hope so. Its starting point was my lecture. And, at that time, I also said that,

に、彼らが言うには「私たちは教育をしているだけである。ウイグル人は、自分たちの文化の教育を受けただけでは、それ以外の中国企業に就職できないし中国の大学に入学もできないので、彼らの教育を変え、中国語を教えることに加えて、中国人としての振る舞い方も訓練しようとしている」ということでしたが、強制収容所の存在自体は認めたのです。

　この問題に関しては、今年３月の台湾の説法でも再び言及しましたし、そのときは香港問題にも触れました。「台湾は台湾であるべきです。一国二制度は機能していません。ですから、あなたがたの自由、民主主義、繁栄を守ってください」とお話ししました。当時は蔡英文の勢いが弱まっていましたが、今は回復しているので、次の選挙も勝っていただきたいと思います。そのきっかけは私の説法でした。その説法では、「どうか香港の人たちを助けてください。彼らが困っているときは助けてく

"Please help Hong Kong people. If they are in trouble, please help them." I said so. Now, Taiwan people are assisting Hong Kong people, indeed. To protect Hong Kong means to protect Taiwan. To protect Taiwan means to protect Japan, and to protect the Philippines or Vietnam or other countries.

Xi Jinping is now traveling around India and Nepal because of trading problem with the United States of America. He wants to make a new way for their trading system. But in these countries already I made a lecture, so they will not change their mind in the main concept. So, we will continue the surrounding-China strategy, continuously.

The end of China: its economic collapse

And I will collapse the economy of Communist Party. It is said that, if the economic growth were less than seven percent, the one-party system will be

ださい」ともお話ししました。今、実際に台湾の人たち
は香港の人たちを支援しています。香港を守ることは台
湾を守ることであり、台湾を守ることは日本を守り、フィ
リピンやベトナムやその他の国を守ることでもあるので
す。

　習近平は今、アメリカとの貿易問題があるため、イン
ドとネパールを回っています。新たな貿易体制のための
道をつけたいわけですが、それらの国は私がすでに巡錫
して説法をしたところなので、中心となる考えを変える
ことはないでしょう。ですから、引き続き中国包囲戦略
を継続していくつもりです。

経済崩壊が「中国の終わり」の時

　そして、共産党下の経済も崩壊させようと思っていま
す。「経済成長が７パーセントを切ったら一党体制は崩
壊する」と言う見方を聞いたことがあります。今、中国

collapsed. I've heard so. Now, they are around six percent economic growth, but this is just a lie. Their development speed is lower than this one, almost the same as Japan or so. So, people will know the reality of their economics.

In the country of China, "What God is" means economic growth. They had been making a great economic growth through these 30 years. This is their religion. This is their faith. Their faith in communism or socialist system is better than American way of capitalism or Japanese way of system. But Mr. Donald Trump already found what happened in these 30 years. And in Japan also, I already found what happened to China and what happened to Japan. I already told a lot about that. It was American policy to help China and make Japan lose, but they changed their mind. They will assist Japanese economy and they will want to ruin Chinese economy. This is the next decade, I surely said so.

の経済成長は6パーセントくらいですが、これは嘘であって、彼らの発展速度は6パーセント以下で日本と変わらないくらいなので、中国の経済学の実態が知られることになるでしょう。

中国という国では、〝神〟とは何かというと、経済成長のことなのです。中国は過去30年間、高度経済成長を続けてきましたが、これが彼らの〝宗教〟であり〝信仰〟なのです。「彼らの共産主義や社会主義制度に対する信仰のほうが、アメリカ的な資本主義や日本式のやり方より優れている」というわけですが、ドナルド・トランプ氏は、この30年間で何が起きたのか、すでに気づいています。日本でも、私がすでに、「中国で何が起き、日本で何が起きたのか」に気づいており、すでにそれについて何度も述べています。それは中国を助け、日本を敗北させるための、アメリカの政策だったわけですが、アメリカはその考えを変えました。アメリカは日本経済を助けて中国経済を崩壊させようとするでしょう。これが「次の10年」であると明言しました。

4 A Message to Fighters Who Have Faith in God

So, they will suffer a worldwide ruin. One Belt, One Road system will be ruined in the near future, and I will, we will ruin them. In this context, "we" includes our Happiness Realization Party; we must make the next strategy for Japanese economic growth, and we must again get the No.2 of the economic level. At that time, it will be the end of communist one-party system, the end of China. I think so. We have such kind of strategy.

Elohim's promise to His people of Uyghur

Ryuho Okawa And this Ms. Rukiye Turdush, she had a deep faith in God. I'll answer her.

This is the voice of Elohim, Your God.
Your Uyghur people's God is here in Japan!
So, I will save you.
I will save you.

ですから中国は、世界規模の崩壊を被ることになるでしょう。一帯一路制度は間もなく破綻すると思います。私が、私たちが破綻させます。「私たち」には幸福実現党も含まれます。私たちは、日本の経済成長のために次なる戦略を立てなければいけませんし、再び世界第二位の経済レベルを取り戻さなければいけません。その時が、「共産党一党独裁体制の終わり」であり、「中国の終わり」になると思います。それが私たちの戦略です。

ウイグル人の神エローヒムの約束

大川隆法　このルキエ・トールダッシュさんは、神への深い信仰をお持ちです。私からお答えします。

　これはあなたがたの神、エローヒムの声です。
　あなたがたウイグル人の神は、この日本にいます！
　ですから、私があなたがたを救います。
　あなたがたを救います。

This is the promise of God!

So, please believe in me!

I will set you free in the near future!

I will do my best,

We will do our best,

And you can continue

Your faith in God.

You will be safe.

I hope so,

I want to do so,

And I will save you.

Kobayashi Thank you so much for your great message. We will make sure that your message will be heard by every single person. Thank you so much.

これは神の約束です！
どうか、私を信じてください！
私は近い将来、あなたがたを自由にします！

私は全力を尽くします。
私たちは全力を尽くします。
そして、あなたがたは
神への信仰を続けることができます。
あなたがたは安全です。
そう願っています。
そうしたいと思います。
私があなたがたを救います。

小林　素晴らしいメッセージをありがとうございます。
必ずや主のメッセージをすべての人に届けてまいります。ありがとうございました。

5 God's Plan and Our Mission

Fujii Thank you for your precious answers to the questions. Lastly, just for your information. On Tuesday this week, it means just two days after the Toronto event, BBC, one of the major TV networks, offered to broadcast *Reigen* (spiritual message) from Margaret Thatcher*.

Ryuho Okawa Margaret Thatcher... OK.

Fujii They asked it to our London *shibucho* (branch manager). She succeeded in promoting Reigen in London. This is very precious information, because I think it means Master made a huge impact in Toronto. So, every British media knows that. I believe so.

---

* Here, he is referring to the spiritual messages from Thatcher given on April 9, 2013, just 19 hours after her death. See Ryuho Okawa, *Margaret Thatcher's Miraculous Message: An Interview with the Iron Lady 19 Hours After Her Death* (New York: IRH Press, 2013).

5　神の計画と私たちの使命

藤井　質問への貴重なお答えを賜り、ありがとうございました。最後にご参考までにお伝えします。今週の火曜日、トロントご講演のわずか2日後に、主要な TV ネットワークである BBC（イギリス国営放送）から、マーガレット・サッチャーの霊言（注）を放送したいと申し出がありました。

大川隆法　マーガレット・サッチャー……はい。

藤井　幸福の科学のロンドン支部長に、そう依頼してきたのです。彼女がロンドンで霊言のプロモーションに成功したのです。これは非常に貴重な情報です。なぜなら、その意味するところは、総裁先生のトロントご講演のインパクトが非常に大きく、イギリスの全メディアもそれを知っているということではないかと思います。

（注）2013 年 4 月 9 日、死後わずか 19 時間後に収録したサッチャーの霊言のこと。『サッチャーのスピリチュアル・メッセージ』（幸福の科学出版刊）参照。

Ryuho Okawa Ah, really? OK. I appreciate it. Yes, we need a new message from Margaret Thatcher or Winston Churchill or the guardian spirit of Boris Johnson in the near future. Next strategy for London or New York, we must make some plan for that.

I'll add that I already predicted the birth of President Mr. Donald Trump in the year of 1989 in my book, *Invincible Thinking*. Almost 30 years ago, firstly. Second is, January of 2016, and next is the autumn, one month before the general election. I predicted the victory of Donald Trump in New York lecture. Even our followers said, "Oh, Master, you should never have said so. We are convinced that Mrs. Clinton will win. It's already fixed, so it's a mistake." They said, but Donald Trump won. It's God's plan.

So, he is required because of the fight against

5　神の計画と私たちの使命

大川隆法　ああ、そうですか。オーケー。ありがたいことです。はい、近いうちに、マーガレット・サッチャーやウィンストン・チャーチルの新しい霊言や、ボリス・ジョンソン守護霊の霊言が必要ですね。ロンドンやニューヨークに向けた次なる戦略として、何か計画を考えないといけません。

　付け加えて言えば、私はすでに1989年に本のなかでドナルド・トランプ大統領の誕生を予言していました。『常勝思考』という本です。30年ほど前で、それが最初でした。二度目は2016年の1月で、その次は（大統領）選挙の1カ月前の秋にニューヨーク説法のなかで、ドナルド・トランプ氏の勝利を予言したのです。当会の信者たちでさえ、「ああ、総裁先生、あれは絶対言わないほうが良かったです。クリントン夫人が勝つに決まってます。もう確定しているので、あれはミスでした」と言っていましたが、ドナルド・トランプが勝ちました。神の計画なのです。

　ですからトランプ氏は、中国と戦うために必要とされ

5 God's Plan and Our Mission

China. He is wanted to fight against China, and we, also, have such kind of mission. So, the future will be brighter. I want to say so. Thank you very much.

5 神の計画と私たちの使命

ているのです。彼は中国と戦うことを求められています
し、私たちにも、そうした使命があります。ですから、「未
来は明るくなる」と申し上げたいと思います。ありがと
うございました。

『いま求められる世界正義』大川隆法著作関連書籍

『太陽の法』
『Love for the Future』
『愛は憎しみを超えて』
『国際政治を見る眼』
『常勝思考』
『自由のために、戦うべきは今』
『習近平守護霊　ウイグル弾圧を語る』
『CO_2 排出削減は正しいか』
『オスカー・ワイルドの霊言』
『サッチャーのスピリチュアル・メッセージ』
（いずれも幸福の科学出版刊）

いま求められる世界正義
—The Reason We Are Here 私たちがここにいる理由—

2019年11月28日　初版第1刷

著　者　　大　川　隆　法

発行所　　幸福の科学出版株式会社

〒107-0052　東京都港区赤坂2丁目10番8号
TEL(03)5573-7700
https://www.irhpress.co.jp/

印刷・製本　　株式会社 堀内印刷所

落丁・乱丁本はおとりかえいたします
©Ryuho Okawa 2019. Printed in Japan. 検印省略
ISBN 978-4-8233-0132-2 C0014
カバー Winning7799/jakkapan/Serz_72/VallaV
帯 Imran Ashraf
以上、Shutterstock.com
装丁・写真（上記・パブリックドメインを除く）© 幸福の科学

大川隆法シリーズ・香港デモ・中国の民主化

愛は憎しみを超えて
中国を民主化させる日本と台湾の使命

中国に台湾の民主主義を広げよ——。この「中台問題」の正論が、第三次世界大戦の勃発をくい止める。台湾と名古屋での講演を収録した著者渾身の一冊。

1,500円

自由のために、戦うべきは今
習近平 vs. アグネス・チョウ
守護霊霊言

今、民主化デモを超えた「香港革命」が起きている。アグネス・チョウ氏と習近平氏の守護霊霊言から、「神の正義」を読む。天草四郎の霊言等も同時収録。

1,400円

ジョシュア・ウォン守護霊の英語霊言
自由を守りぬく覚悟

英語霊言 日本語訳付き

勇気、自己犠牲の精神、そして、自由への願い——。22歳の香港デモリーダー、ジョシュア・ウォン氏の守護霊が語る、香港民主化の願いと日本への期待。

1,400円

幸福の科学出版

大川隆法 公開霊言シリーズ

サッチャーの
スピリチュアル・メッセージ
死後19時間での奇跡のインタビュー

フォークランド紛争、英国病、景気回復……。
勇気を持って数々の難問を解決し、イギリス
を繁栄に導いたサッチャー元首相が、日本に
アドバイス！

1,300円

オスカー・ワイルドの霊言

ほんとうの愛と LGBT 問題

世界で広がるLGBTの新しい波。同性愛はど
こまで許されるのか。真の愛、真の美とは
何であるのか。イギリス世紀末文学の代表
的作家が、死後119年目の本心を語る。

1,400円

イエス・キリストに聞く
「同性婚問題」

性と愛を巡って

時代の揺らぎか？ 新しい愛のカタチか？
同性婚や同性愛は、果たして宗教的に認め
られるのか──。天上界から語られる、イエ
スの衝撃のメッセージ。

1,400円

※表示価格は本体価格（税別）です。

大川隆法シリーズ・最新刊

CO_2 排出削減は正しいか
なぜ、グレタは怒っているのか？

英語霊言
日本語訳付き

国連で「怒りのスピーチ」をした16歳の少女の主張は、本当に正しいのか？ グレタ氏に影響を与える霊存在や、気候変動と二酸化炭素の因果関係などが明らかに。

1,400円

道なき道を歩め
未来へ貢献する心

未来文明の源流となる学校・HSU。英語や人間関係力、経営成功法などを学び、世界に羽ばたく人材へ──。2018年度卒業式の法話も収録。【HSU出版会刊】

1,500円

生霊論
運命向上の智慧と秘術

それは、あなたの毎日に影響を与えている、目に見えない力──。生霊にまつわるあらゆる事象をズバッと解説。「生霊に影響されない」「自分が生霊にならない」対策とは。

1,600円

幸福の科学出版

大川隆法「法シリーズ」

青銅の法
人類のルーツに目覚め、愛に生きる

法シリーズ第25作

限りある人生のなかで、
永遠の真理をつかむ——。
地球の起源と未来、宇宙の神秘、
そして「愛」の持つ力を明かした、
待望の法シリーズ最新刊。

第1章 情熱の高め方
—— 無私のリーダーシップを目指す生き方
第2章 自己犠牲の精神
—— 世のため人のために尽くす生き方
第3章 青銅の扉
—— 現代の国際社会で求められる信仰者の生き方
第4章 宇宙時代の幕開け
—— 自由、民主、信仰を広げるミッションに生きる
第5章 愛を広げる力
—— あなたを突き動かす「神の愛」のエネルギー

2,000円

ワールド・ティーチャーが贈る「不滅の真理」

「仏法真理の全体像」と「新時代の価値観」を示す法シリーズ！
全国書店にて好評発売中！

※表示価格は本体価格(税別)です。

出会えたひと、すべてが宝物。

限りある人生を、あなたはどう生きますか？
世代を超えた心のふれあいから、「生きるって何？」を描きだす。

ドキュメンタリー映画
光り合う生命。
いのち
―心に寄り添う。2―

企画／大川隆法
メインテーマ「光り合う生命。」挿入歌「青春の輝き」作詞・作曲／大川隆法

出演／希島 凛　渡辺優凜　監督／奥津貴之　音楽／水澤有一　製作／ARI Production　配給／東京テアトル　©2019 ARI Production

全国の幸福の科学支部・精舎で公開中！

——真実は、絶対に死なない。

世界から希望が消えたなら。

世界で25冠

サンディエゴ国際映画祭 2019
ワールド・プレミア賞ノミネート

マドリード国際映画祭2019 外国語映画部門
最優秀監督賞 受賞

マドリード国際映画祭 2019　外国語映画部門　最優秀作品賞ノミネート／フローレンス映画賞 2019(7月度)長編部門名誉賞受賞／フローレンス映画賞 2019(7月度)脚本賞受賞／アウェアネス映画祭 2019　功労賞受賞／バルセロナ国際映画祭 2019 カステル賞受賞／インディ・ビジョンズ映画祭 2019(7月度)物語部門受賞／ダイヤモンド映画祭 2019(7月度)物語部門受賞／ザ・サウス映画芸術祭 2019(8月度)長編部門　名誉主演男優賞受賞／ザ・サウス映画芸術祭 2019(8月度)長編部門　最優秀ファンタジー賞受賞／ザ・サウス映画芸術祭 2019(8月度)長編部門　名誉監督賞受賞／ザ・サウス映画芸術祭 2019(8月度)長編部門　名誉脚本賞受賞／ザ・サウス映画芸術祭 2019(8月度)長編部門　名誉オリジナル楽曲賞受賞／ザ・サウス映画芸術祭 2019(8月度)長編部門　名誉プロダクション賞受賞／ザ・サウス映画芸術祭 2019(8月度)長編部門　名誉美術監督賞受賞／ザ・サウス映画芸術祭 2019(8月度)長編部門　最優秀 VFX 賞受賞／フェスティジャス映画祭 2019(8月度)最優秀原作賞受賞／フェスティジャス映画祭 2019(8月度)最優秀作品賞受賞／フェスティジャス映画祭 2019(8月度)最優秀長編物語賞受賞／フェスティジャス映画祭 2019(8月度)最優秀インスピレーション賞受賞／ CKF 国際映画祭 2019(8月度)最優秀長編作品賞受賞／ CKF 国際映画祭 2019(8月度)最優秀海外主演男優賞受賞／コルカタ国際カルト映画祭 2019(8月度)物語部門　功績賞受賞／ゴールデン・アース映画賞 2019(9月度)脚本賞受賞／マンスリー映画祭 2019 10月度　予告編賞受賞／ベスト・アクター・アワード 2019 9 ～ 10月度　最優秀初主演男優部門 プラチナ賞受賞　※ 11月時点

製作総指揮・原案　大川隆法

竹内久顕　千眼美子　さとう珠緒

芦川よしみ　石橋保　木下渓　小倉一郎　大浦龍宇一　河相我聞　田村亮

監督／赤羽博　音楽／水澤有一　脚本／大川咲也加

製作／幸福の科学出版　製作協力／ ARI Production　ニュースター・プロダクション

制作プロダクション／ジャンゴフィルム　配給／日活　配給協力／東京テアトル　©2019 IRH Press　sekai-kibou.jp

10.18

大ヒット上映中

幸福の科学グループのご案内

宗教、教育、政治、出版などの活動を通じて、地球的ユートピアの実現を目指しています。

幸福の科学

1986年に立宗。信仰の対象は、地球系霊団の最高大霊、主エル・カンターレ。世界100カ国以上の国々に信者を持ち、全人類救済という尊い使命のもと、信者は、「愛」と「悟り」と「ユートピア建設」の教えの実践、伝道に励んでいます。

（2019年11月現在）

愛　　幸福の科学の「愛」とは、与える愛です。これは、仏教の慈悲や布施の精神と同じことです。信者は、仏法真理をお伝えすることを通して、多くの方に幸福な人生を送っていただくための活動に励んでいます。

悟り　「悟り」とは、自らが仏の子であることを知るということです。教学や精神統一によって心を磨き、智慧を得て悩みを解決すると共に、天使・菩薩の境地を目指し、より多くの人を救える力を身につけていきます。

ユートピア建設　私たち人間は、地上に理想世界を建設するという尊い使命を持って生まれてきています。社会の悪を押しとどめ、善を推し進めるために、信者はさまざまな活動に積極的に参加しています。

国内外の世界で貧困や災害、心の病で苦しんでいる人々に対しては、現地メンバーや支援団体と連携して、物心両面にわたり、あらゆる手段で手を差し伸べています。

年間約2万人の自殺者を減らすため、全国各地で街頭キャンペーンを展開しています。

公式サイト www.withyou-hs.net

ヘレン・ケラーを理想として活動する、ハンディキャップを持つ方とボランティアの会です。視聴覚障害者、肢体不自由な方々に仏法真理を学んでいただくための、さまざまなサポートをしています。

公式サイト www.helen-hs.net

入会のご案内

幸福の科学では、大川隆法総裁が説く仏法真理(ぶっぽうしんり)をもとに、「どうすれば幸福になれるのか、また、他の人を幸福にできるのか」を学び、実践しています。

入会 — 仏法真理を学んでみたい方へ

大川隆法総裁の教えを信じ、学ぼうとする方なら、どなたでも入会できます。入会された方には、『入会版「正心法語(しょうしんほうご)」』が授与されます。

ネット入会 入会ご希望の方はネットからも入会できます。

happy-science.jp/joinus

三帰(さんき)誓願(せいがん) — 信仰をさらに深めたい方へ

仏弟子としてさらに信仰を深めたい方は、仏・法・僧の三宝(ぶっぽうそうさんぼう)への帰依を誓う「三帰誓願式」を受けることができます。三帰誓願者には、『仏説・正心法語』『祈願文(きがんもん)①』『祈願文②』『エル・カンターレへの祈り』が授与されます。

幸福の科学 サービスセンター
TEL 03-5793-1727
受付時間/
火〜金:10〜20時
土・日祝:10〜18時
(月曜を除く)

幸福の科学 公式サイト
happy-science.jp

幸福の科学グループの教育・人材養成事業

教育 HSU ハッピー・サイエンス・ユニバーシティ
Happy Science University

ハッピー・サイエンス・ユニバーシティとは

ハッピー・サイエンス・ユニバーシティ(HSU)は、大川隆法総裁が設立された
「現代の松下村塾」であり、「日本発の本格私学」です。
建学の精神として「幸福の探究と新文明の創造」を掲げ、
チャレンジ精神にあふれ、新時代を切り拓く人材の輩出を目指します。

| 人間幸福学部 | 経営成功学部 | 未来産業学部 |

HSU長生キャンパス TEL **0475-32-7770**
〒299-4325　千葉県長生郡長生村一松丙 4427-1

| 未来創造学部 |

HSU未来創造・東京キャンパス
TEL **03-3699-7707**
〒136-0076　東京都江東区南砂2-6-5　公式サイト **happy-science.university**

学校法人 幸福の科学学園

学校法人 幸福の科学学園は、幸福の科学の教育理念のもとにつくられた教育機関です。人間にとって最も大切な宗教教育の導入を通じて精神性を高めながら、ユートピア建設に貢献する人材輩出を目指しています。

幸福の科学学園
中学校・高等学校（那須本校）
2010年4月開校・栃木県那須郡（男女共学・全寮制）
TEL **0287-75-7777**　公式サイト **happy-science.ac.jp**

関西中学校・高等学校（関西校）
2013年4月開校・滋賀県大津市（男女共学・寮及び通学）
TEL **077-573-7774**　公式サイト **kansai.happy-science.ac.jp**

幸福の科学グループの教育・人材養成事業

仏法真理塾「サクセスNo.1」

全国に本校・拠点・支部校を展開する、幸福の科学による信仰教育の機関です。小学生・中学生・高校生を対象に、信仰教育・徳育にウエイトを置きつつ、将来、社会人として活躍するための学力養成にも力を注いでいます。

TEL 03-5750-0751（東京本校）

エンゼルプランV　**TEL 03-5750-0757**
幼少時からの心の教育を大切にして、信仰をベースにした幼児教育を行っています。

不登校児支援スクール「ネバー・マインド」　**TEL 03-5750-1741**
心の面からのアプローチを重視して、不登校の子供たちを支援しています。

ユー・アー・エンゼル！（あなたは天使！）運動
一般社団法人 ユー・アー・エンゼル　**TEL 03-6426-7797**
障害児の不安や悩みに取り組み、ご両親を励まし、勇気づける、
障害児支援のボランティア運動を展開しています。

NPO活動支援

学校からのいじめ追放を目指し、さまざまな社会提言をしています。また、各地でのシンポジウムや学校への啓発ポスター掲示等に取り組む一般財団法人「いじめから子供を守ろうネットワーク」を支援しています。

公式サイト mamoro.org　**ブログ** blog.mamoro.org
相談窓口 TEL.03-5544-8989

百歳まで生きる会

「百歳まで生きる会」は、生涯現役人生を掲げ、友達づくり、生きがいづくりをめざしている幸福の科学のシニア信者の集まりです。

シニア・プラン21

生涯反省で人生を再生・新生し、希望に満ちた生涯現役人生を生きる仏法真理道場です。定期的に開催される研修には、年齢を問わず、多くの方が参加しています。全世界211カ所（国内196カ所、海外15カ所）で開校中。

【東京校】**TEL 03-6384-0778**　**FAX 03-6384-0779**
メール senior-plan@kofuku-no-kagaku.or.jp

幸福の科学グループ事業

政治

幸福実現党

幸福実現党 釈量子サイト
shaku-ryoko.net

Twitter
釈量子@shakuryoko
で検索

党の機関紙
「幸福実現NEWS」

ないゆうがいかん
内憂外患の国難に立ち向かうべく、2009年5月に幸福実現党を立党しました。創立者である大川隆法党総裁の精神的指導のもと、宗教だけでは解決できない問題に取り組み、幸福を具体化するための力になっています。

幸福実現党 党員募集中

あなたも幸福を実現する政治に参画しませんか。

○ 幸福実現党の理念と綱領、政策に賛同する18歳以上の方なら、どなたでも参加いただけます。
○ 党費：正党員（年額5千円［学生 年額2千円］）、特別党員（年額10万円以上）、家族党員（年額2千円）
○ 党員資格は党費を入金された日から1年間です。
○ 正党員、特別党員の皆様には機関紙「幸福実現NEWS（党員版）」（不定期発行）が送付されます。

＊申込書は、下記、幸福実現党公式サイトでダウンロードできます。
住所：〒107-0052　東京都港区赤坂2-10-8 6階 幸福実現党本部

TEL 03-6441-0754　　FAX 03-6441-0764
公式サイト　hr-party.jp

幸福の科学グループ事業

幸福の科学出版

出版メディア事業

大川隆法総裁の仏法真理の書を中心に、ビジネス、自己啓発、小説など、さまざまなジャンルの書籍・雑誌を出版しています。他にも、映画事業、文学・学術発展のための振興事業、テレビ・ラジオ番組の提供など、幸福の科学文化を広げる事業を行っています。

アー・ユー・ハッピー？
are-you-happy.com

ザ・リバティ
the-liberty.com

ザ・ファクト
マスコミが報道しない「事実」を世界に伝えるネット・オピニオン番組

YouTubeにて随時好評配信中！

ザ・ファクト　検索

幸福の科学出版
TEL 03-5573-7700
公式サイト irhpress.co.jp

ニュースター・プロダクション

芸能文化事業

「新時代の美」を創造する芸能プロダクションです。多くの方々に良き感化を与えられるような魅力あふれるタレントを世に送り出すべく、日々、活動しています。

公式サイト newstarpro.co.jp

ARI Production
（アリプロダクション）

タレント一人ひとりの個性や魅力を引き出し、「新時代を創造するエンターテインメント」をコンセプトに、世の中に精神的価値のある作品を提供していく芸能プロダクションです。

公式サイト aripro.co.jp

大川隆法　講演会のご案内

大川隆法総裁の講演会が全国各地で開催されています。講演のなかでは、毎回、「世界教師」としての立場から、幸福な人生を生きるための心の教えをはじめ、世界各地で起きている宗教対立、紛争、国際政治や経済といった時事問題に対する指針など、日本と世界がさらなる繁栄の未来を実現するための道筋が示されています。

2019年5月14日 幕張メッセ「自由・民主・信仰の世界」

2019年10月6日 ザ ウェスティン ハーバー キャッスル トロント(カナダ)「The Reason We Are Here」

2019年3月3日 グランド ハイアット 台北(台湾)「愛は憎しみを超えて」

2019年7月5日 福岡国際センター「人生に自信を持て」

2019年7月13日 ホテル イースト21 東京「幸福への論点」

講演会には、どなたでもご参加いただけます。
最新の講演会の開催情報はこちらへ。　➡　大川隆法総裁公式サイト
https://ryuho-okawa.org